Rising Above the Wave

Rising
Above
the Wave

**Surviving Tsunami and
Stroke in Japan 2011**

Walt Christie

Designed and Produced by
Maine Authors Publishing
558 Main Street, Rockland, Maine 04841
www.maineauthorspublishing.com

To Ellie,

whose clear mind, courage, hard work, and love
have made this book possible.

Contents

I

A Strange Force Crosses the Pacific

On March 10, 2011, at 9:30 p.m., a Thai Airlines passenger jet will take off from Los Angeles International Airport on a nonstop flight to Bangkok, Thailand. Walt and Ellie Christie will be among the passengers. In Bangkok, they will board a smaller plane for Paro, Bhutan, to meet the rest of their party for hiking and sightseeing.

Ellie is passionately interested in Tibetan Buddhism, particularly the teachings of the Dalai Lama. His works had sparked a journey with Ginny, a friend who shares her enthusiasms. In 1988, the two women hiked through the breathtaking Himalayan mountain ranges of Nepal before going on to Tibet. Now another friend, Judith Meyers, has put together a group of congenial people from all over the country to travel to Bhutan. Walt and Ellie are excited to be returning to a Tibetan Buddhist country.

While boarding the plane, Walt has trepidations. From Los Angeles to Bangkok is a nineteen-hour flight, and he and Ellie have not made a similar one since their trip to India and Nepal in 1995. Walt is particularly anxious, since sleeping on airplanes is difficult for him.

The big plane fills up, and Walt and Ellie find their seats. Most of the passengers, as well as the flight attendants, are Thai. When they are settled in their seats, Walt takes a sleeping pill, and before long he falls asleep with his head against the window. Ellie is awake for a while, but then starts to doze. The plane heads northwest along the Aleutian Islands and then over the ocean, heading for Asia.

On March 11, 2011, at 2:46 p.m., fifteen minutes after the plane has taken off, an earthquake starts off the island of Honshu about 45 miles east of Tokohu. The mega-thrust 9+ earthquake, the biggest in Japan's modern history, is felt from the fjords of Norway to the Antarctic ice sheet. It is triggered at a depth of 20 miles when the Pacific tectonic plate lets go and dives beneath the Eurasian plate, releasing tremendous tension. The sea floor rises up 30 feet to produce an enormous tsunami with its crest topping 128 feet. In the process, it floods 217 miles of Japan coastline and will kill and drown over 18,000 people.

Tokyo, the most seismic-sensitive of urban areas, puts out a one-minute warning. High-speed trains and buses stop, and people scurry for shelter. Although Tokyo is well prepared, with about 1,000 quakes per year, this quake is the largest. In villages to the north of Tokyo, dogs bark an eerie warning, and then glass breaks, walls and ceilings collapse, and fires start. The shaking continues for about six minutes, and any building that cannot tolerate the agitation is destroyed. More than 250 miles of Honshu coastline drop by two feet, and the whole island moves eight feet eastward.

Walt and Ellie's plane is flying at 600 mph, and the tsunami wave rushes forward at 400 mph. It is not so much a wave as a cataclysmic force, traveling through the water and bending around any land it meets. In 12 hours the tsunami will slam into the coast of North America, and in 24 hours it will wash down the coast of Chili. Unaware of its presence, the plane meets the tsunami head-on, and plane and tsunami continue in opposite directions.

The plane and the wave pass one another, and Ellie jerks awake. She anxiously looks at Walt, who is slumped against the window. His face seems wrong, distorted. She leans forward and peers closer. The right half of his face is drooping. She gently shakes him. He turns slightly, and instantly she recognizes the signs.

"Are you having a stroke?" she says, anticipating the worst.

Walt nods feebly. He cannot move. He is paralyzed on his right side. Ellie quickly finds a flight attendant.

"My husband is having a stroke," she says to the attendant.

Confused by language, the hostess asks if Walt has a headache. Ellie interrupts her.

"Please get a doctor," she says. "Is there one on the plane?"

Inside Fukushima Daiichi Nuclear Power Plant, the initial tremors of the earthquake damage the pipes that carry coolant to the nuclear reactors. By the second major tremor, the pipes have loosened and are bursting open. In Reactor 1, oxygen tanks explode, while overhead pipes jerk away from the walls. The emergency team is mobilized, and enclosed in white hazmat suits, they struggle to repair the broken pipes. Thick white smoke comes from the top of Reactor 1, and it starts to collapse.

There is no time to repair the damage because 51 minutes after the first tremor, the tsunami is gathering into a huge trough. All along the northeast coast of Japan, the ocean drains back...and then it comes rushing forward in an unremitting surge, dragging the bottom of the sea with it. Although the prudent Japanese have built 21-foot-high tsunami walls, water spills 6 meters over them, and it keeps on coming, crushing the weakest buildings like matchsticks. Boats break free of their moorings, then swirl and break apart with the power of the wave.

The tsunami wave mortally injures five workers as it bashes the sides of Reactors 1 and 2 and floods basements, cutting off all power to the emergency diesel generators. The backup generators, installed in a watertight building up the hillside, lose their power and fail. A meltdown is inevitable.

As the ocean pours over the tsunami wall, huge fishing boats spin onto buildings, where their keels catch on rooftops and hang there. The citizens try to flee, but the streets are inundated by 20 feet of water. Those fortunate enough to scramble to the rooftops see a huge wave of gasoline, diesel, and blood-saturated water sweeping around them. Everywhere, bodies are floating.

At Fukushima, the water rises 49 feet, and the temperatures continue to go up. Reactors 1, 2, 3, and 4 experience meltdowns, exposing the fuel rods. One worker, when he puts his foot on the valve, hears "an eerie, deep popping noise," and his rubber boot melts from the heat.

On the intercom, the pilot pages for a doctor. Two physicians hear the call and come forward. One, an obstetrician, realizes that he lacks the skill to deal with a stroke victim and excuses himself to return to his seat. The other, Dr. Jordan Waldman, a pediatric anesthesiologist, has experience stabilizing patients in the operating room. Jordan has a pleasant, calm manner, and, like most physicians, he puts his emotions on the shelf.

Jordan is directed to where Ellie is cradling Walt. She tells him that Walt has had a stroke, and Jordan notes that Walt has paralysis on the right side, and he is drooling. There is no question about the diagnosis—a stroke.

Jordan asks the attendant to bring an emergency kit, and with it he takes Walt's blood pressure and pulse. Walt's heart rate is in the 70s, and Jordan hooks up an EKG. Ellie tells him that Walt is a healthy person with no predispositions. This stroke is totally unforeseen.

Jordan is impressed with Ellie's demeanor. It is clear that she loves Walt deeply, yet she is calm, clear, goal-oriented, and alert to all around her. He has seldom met a person who combines her sense of compassion with a clear focus for action.

To prevent Walt from getting dehydrated Jordan starts a saline IV and gives him an aspirin to prevent his blood from clotting. Then he confers with Ellie. Both know that TPA (Tissue Plasminogen Activator) should be administered, but it is not available on the plane and, regardless, should be given within two hours of having a stroke. Tokyo is at least three hours away. If they land there, will anything be done for Walt? On the other hand, if they continue another ten hours to Thailand, Walt could die on the airplane.

Jordan goes to the cockpit to talk with the captain, while Ellie holds Walt close. She knows that she must breathe deeply and concentrate on what they will both face, whatever that may be.

On his way to the cockpit, Jordan checks with his wife, Anita, who supports his course of action. Feeling less alone, Jordan continues to the front. On reaching the cockpit, Jordan talks with the crew chief, and they decide to call the airline's medical consultant, who is located in Bangkok. After getting the details of Walt's condition, the consultant, who sounds like an American, agrees with Jordan that the plane should land.

At this point, no one, including the captain, knows about the earthquake or realizes that landing in Japan will be extremely problematic. As they approach Japan, planes from Delta, American Airlines, United, and Air Canada, as well as those of Al Nippon and Japan Air Lines, are circling Tokyo in holding patterns and watching their fuel diminish. Meanwhile, the anxious Japanese controllers offer flimsy excuses such as Narita (Tokyo) airport is "closed for inspection," but "expected to open soon." No one talks over the airwaves about the earthquake and tsunami.

Jordan tells the crew chief that landing is necessary, and the captain begins his descent into Tokyo. Suddenly he is told to hold. The captain cannot help but notice the large number of planes holding with him, and he grows increasingly concerned. He has a critically ill man on the plane, but controllers are telling him that the holding time for Narita is "indefinite."

Behind him in line, a new Delta pilot is trying to figure out what to do. Later, he writes:

> I'm currently still in one piece, writing from my room in the Narita crew hotel. It's 8 a.m. This is my inaugural trans-pacific trip as a brand new, recently checked out, international 767 Captain and it has been interesting, to say the least so far. I've crossed the Atlantic three times so far so the ocean crossing procedures were familiar.
>
> By the way, stunning scenery flying over the Aleutian Islands. Everything was going fine until 100 miles out from Tokyo and in the descent for arrival. The first indication of any trouble was that Japan air traffic control started putting

everyone into holding patterns. At first we thought it was usual congestion on arrival. Then we got a company data link message advising about the earthquake, followed by another stating Narita airport was temporarily closed for inspection and expected to open shortly (the company is always so positive).

From our perspective, things were obviously looking a little different. The Japanese controller's anxiety level seemed quite high and he said expect "indefinite" holding time. No one would commit to a time frame on that, so I got my copilot and relief pilot busy looking at divert stations and our fuel situation, which, after an ocean crossing is typically low.

It wasn't long, maybe ten minutes, before the first pilots started requesting diversions to other airports. Air Canada, American, United, etc., all reporting minimal fuel situations. I still had enough fuel for 1.5 to 2.0 hours of holding. Needless to say, the diverts started complicating the situation.

Japan air traffic control then announced Narita was closed indefinitely due to damage. Planes immediately started requesting arrivals into Haneda, near Tokyo; a half dozen JAL and western planes got clearance in that direction, but then ATC announced Haneda had just closed. Uh-oh! Now instead of just holding, we all had to start looking at more distant alternatives like Osaka, or Nagoya.

One bad thing about a large airliner is that you can't just be-bop into any little airport. We generally need lots of runway. With more planes piling in from both east and west, all needing a place to land and several now fuel critical, ATC was getting overwhelmed. In the scramble, and without waiting for my fuel to get critical, I got my flight a clearance to head for Nagoya, fuel situation still okay. So far, so good. A few minutes into heading that way, I was "ordered" by ATC to reverse course. Nagoya was saturated with traffic and unable to handle more planes (read: airport full). Ditto for Osaka.

With that statement, my situation went instantly from fuel okay to fuel minimal, considering we might have to divert a much farther distance. Multiply my situation by a dozen other aircraft all in the same boat, all making demands, requests, and threats to ATC for clearances somewhere. Air Canada and then someone else went to "emergency" fuel situation. Planes started heading for air force bases. The nearest to Tokyo was Yokoda AFB. I threw my hat in the ring for that initially. The answer—Yokoda closed! No more space.

By now it was a three-ring circus in the cockpit, my copilot on the radios, me flying and making decisions, and the relief copilot buried in the air charts trying to figure out where to go that was within range while data link messages were flying back and forth between us and company dispatch in Atlanta. I picked Misawa AFB at the north end of Honshu Island. We could get there with minimal fuel remaining. ATC was happy to get rid of us, so we cleared out of the maelstrom of the Tokyo region. We heard ATC try to send planes toward Sendai, a small regional airport on the coast, which was later the one I think that got flooded by a tsunami.

Atlanta dispatch then sent us a message asking if we could continue to Chitose airport on the Island of Hokkaido, north of Honshu. Other Delta planes were heading that way. More scrambling in the cockpit—check weather, check charts, check fuel, okay. We could still make it and not be going into a fuel critical situation...if we had no other fuel delays. As we approached Misawa, we got clearance to continue to Chitose. Critical decision thought process. Let's see—trying to help company—plane overflies perfectly good divert airport for one farther away...wonder how that will look in the safety report, if anything goes wrong.

Suddenly ATC comes up and gives us a vector to a fix well short of Chitose and tells us to stand by for holding instructions. Nightmare realized. Situation rapidly deteriorating. After initially holding near Tokyo, starting a divert to Nagoya, reversing course back to Tokyo then re-diverting north toward Misawa, all that happy fuel reserve that I had was vaporizing fast. My subsequent conversation, paraphrased of course, went something like this:

"Sapporo Control—Delta XX requesting immediate clearance direct to Chitose, minimum fuel, unable hold."

"Negative Ghost-Rider, the pattern is full."

"Sapporo Control—make that—Delta XX declaring emergency, low fuel, proceeding direct Chitose."

"Roger, Delta XX, understood, you are cleared direct to Chitose, contact Chitose approach…, etc…."

Enough was enough, I had decided to preempt actually running critically low on fuel while in another indefinite holding pattern, especially after bypassing Misawa, and played my last ace…declaring an emergency. The problem with that is now I have a bit of company paperwork to do, but what the heck.

As it was—landed Chitose, safe, with at least 30 minutes of fuel remaining before reaching a "true" fuel emergency situation. That's always a good feeling, being safe. They taxied us off to some remote parking area where we shut down and watched a half dozen or more other airplanes come streaming in. In the end, Delta had two 747s, my 767 and another 767, and a 777 all on the ramp at Chitose. We saw two American airlines planes, a United, and two Air Canada as well. Not to mention several extra Al Nippon and Japan Air Lines planes.

Post-script: 9 hours later, Japan Air Lines finally got around to getting a boarding ladder to the plane, where we were able to get off and clear customs. That, however, is another interesting story.

By the way—while writing this—I have felt four additional tremors that shook the hotel slightly—all in 45 minutes.

Cheers, J.D.

≈

It is very quiet in the cabin of the plane. The passengers seem to recognize that Walt's illness is serious. Ellie reassures him that she is right there for him. Jordan tells Ellie that the captain has decided to land in Tokyo. There, he says, she can take Walt to a good hospital where, perhaps, there might be time to give him TPA.

Suddenly, a staff member approaches Jordan and tells him that they cannot land in Tokyo because the "runways are breaking up." Ground control still will not acknowledge that there has been an earthquake.

The cabin remains very quiet. People are respectful. Everyone is unaware that they have crossed the track of a fast-moving tsunami and that below them an enormous earthquake is causing extensive damage to the country of Japan. All they know is that a critically ill man is on their plane, which seems to be having difficulty making an emergency landing in Japan.

It is night when the plane finally lands in Osaka. Quickly, white-masked paramedics come on board and examine Walt. They ask Ellie and Jordan for history. The other passengers sit quietly as the paramedics place Walt on a gurney and take him down the aisle. Passengers by the aisle stand and bow to Walt and Ellie as they pass.

Ellie reluctantly says goodbye to Jordan, who has been of immense help, and she goes down the steps after the paramedics. They put Walt in an ambulance. Meanwhile, Ellie meets the ground services representative. In a starched suit with her hair pulled back in a bun, the Thai woman efficiently tells Ellie in English that they are going to the Rinku General Medical Center. Ellie nods and gets in the ambulance with Walt. Through the dim gray city they travel, and she thinks, I must gather all my strength for what lies ahead. The representative's pager buzzes with one request after another. Finally, overwhelmed by all the tasks surfacing, she loses her composure and tells Ellie of the earthquake and tsunami.

When they get to the hospital, the ground services representative offers to send an e-mail to a family member. Ellie gives her the address of Walt's son, Robert, who lives in Hong Kong. Before the representative can leave, Ellie asks her if the luggage, which contains all the trekking gear, is all right left in the waiting room. The woman is quite shocked.

"Of course; this is Japan!" she says.

Meanwhile, Walt is taken for an MRI, and Ellie is told to wait.

Eventually a young resident comes to explain to her, in his two or three words of English, that Walt has had a stroke. He shows Ellie the MRI, where she sees a lesion in the basilar area of the brain. By this time, Walt has been given some miso soup and custard. He tries to use his left hand with the miso soup, but gags and coughs. Finally the dietary aide takes the food away.

Ellie accompanies him as an orderly pushes him on a stretcher to his room. The nurses remove Walt's clothes and help him get into a Johnny. They prepare a narrow bed for him that has a series of sheets that he is instructed to lie in quietly. When they have ensured that he will not move in the bed, they gesture to Ellie that, at least for the rest of the night, she may sleep on a small cot in a window seat. They bring her a pillow and a blanket.

The nurse turns the lights out, and Ellie sits in the dark. She is together with her impaired husband in a hospital where no one speaks English. They are in a country that is coming apart from a catastrophic earthquake and tsunami.

At Fukushima nuclear plant, radiation spews out as workers try to control the catastrophically leaking plant. Evening approaches, and the plant manager decides to start pumping seawater to cool the reactors. However, several hydrogen explosions occur, injuring four more workers and causing what will be the worst radiation contamination in maritime history.

In the next two days, reports of meltdowns will be guarded, and casualties will be grossly underestimated at 1,600, tops. In truth, there have been several meltdowns in the short time that Walt and Ellie have been at the hospital, and the ultimate death toll from the tsunami alone will be closer to 18,000.

2

Alone

Ellie sits in the darkness of the quiet hospital, and she cannot tell if Walt is asleep. She feels totally alone. No one speaks English, and she is unable to reach family by phone or e-mail. Walt is paralyzed and cannot speak. Realizing how dire their situation is, she takes a deep breath, closes her eyes, and wills the clear, calm mind the Dalai Lama teaches. She thinks, I must be fully present and aware in the moment and not cry, because if I do, I might never stop.

Walt lies still in the bed with an IV in his arm. Nurses have started a drip of argatroban, an anticoagulant and small-molecule thrombin inhibitor. After 24 hours, they will add edaravone, a neurological antioxidant that scavenges free radicals and protects against cell death. Ellie gets up and walks to Walt's side. He turns his face slightly toward her, gives a faint smile, and drifts away.

At dawn, hospital staff enter patients' rooms. A dietary services member brings Walt his breakfast, which once again is miso soup. Again Walt chokes on it, so when the woman returns to collect the dishes, Ellie gestures that he should have something other than the soup. It is clear, however, that the woman does not understand her.

It is time for morning rounds, and the resident doctor enters. As he examines Walt, his manner is self-conscious and formal. Ellie, who has spent most of her career teaching young doctors, tries to make eye contact with him, but he resists.

The nurse enters to check Walt's bed and says something in Japanese. Seemingly perturbed, she remakes the bed and motions Walt to lie perfectly still. When she has gone, Ellie tells Walt that she must find the hotel and check in. "I will be back as soon as I can," she explains. Walt nods, appearing to understand.

Ellie walks outside into the large gray Pacific-rim city. It is overcast, windy, and cold, and she is face to face with the Hanshin Expressway, four lanes jammed with black cars whizzing past her. There is no obvious crossing, and the cars do not slow down. On the skyline, the top of the tallest building is swaying back and forth, registering the aftershocks of the earthquake. Dressed all in black, Ellie does not know how she will cross this street safely.

She waits for a break in the traffic and starts across, all the time looking for the next black car that will come racing down upon her. It takes what seems to be an enormous time to cross four lanes, but she reaches the opposite curb and walks to the Kansai Airport Washington Hotel. Inside, she explains to the desk clerk that the airline has made a reservation for her, and then she inquires about the availability of Internet. The desk clerk says theirs is down, but perhaps it is available at the Gateway Towers, the large hotel down the street. She is anxious to get to the Internet to see if Robert has replied to the Thai airline representative. He should have received the e-mail, because today is Saturday, the day after the earthquake.

She is shown to her room, a simple accommodation with a window that looks across the Expressway at the hospital. She checks the closet where she will store their four bags and then goes downstairs. She enters the street and walks toward the Gateway Towers, but finds that the Expressway blocks her. The traffic looks impossible, but finally she finds an overpass. To cross, she must climb up a long flight of stairs to a walkway that goes over the highway. After traversing it, she must descend another flight of stairs to reach the hotel.

The Gateway Towers is a tall building, cylindrical in shape with the Expressway roaring through its base. The black cars, zipping back and forth through the center of the building, are very menacing. The top many stories of the hotel are swaying with the aftershocks. Ellie enters the lobby and looks around for someone who might help her. A young man with gold braid on his suit is standing nearby. Ellie imagines him more comfortable in jeans and a T-shirt and working on his computer. She has her iPad with her and walks up to him.

"Do you speak English?" she asks him, and he waves his hands to signify "no."

Then she points to the iPad, and his eyes light up. She extends the iPad toward him, and he cannot quite believe that she wants him to take it. She signals that she needs the Internet, but he acts as if there is some sort of problem with her request. She is not sure whether this hotel's Internet is down, or something else worries him. However, he gets her meaning and rapidly punches in the code. Ellie's e-mails appear, but the messages are just ordinary, no communication from Robert or anyone else.

This young man is a geek, literate with the computer. Would he, Ellie gestures, help her send an e-mail? He nods affirmatively, so she sits in the lobby and composes an e-mail for the family.

In the early hours of Saturday morning, Robert, sitting at his computer in his home about an hour from Hong Kong, receives a curious message. It is sent at 4:10:19 on March 12 from a J. Kumi, who says, "Please contact your step-mother. She stays in Japan." Ellie's e-mail address is listed on the bottom. Robert almost deletes it, but then he reads it over again. He has Walt's and Ellie's itinerary and knows that they were flying directly to Bangkok yesterday. He can think of no reason that they would be in Japan, especially due to the earthquake and tsunami that happened about 12 hours before. He reads the cryptic e-mail again and then reads it over about twenty times before finally deciding it may be legitimate. To be sure, he e-mails Nirvana Expeditions, the travel agency in Bhutan, his sister Maggie in Boston, and Sandy, his step-sister in Maine.

At 2:40 p.m. on Saturday, Ellie prepares an e-mail to the family. It reads as follows:

Dear Family,

My apologies for e-mailing this very bad news, but I am unable to call. I will still try to reach Rob by phone.

During last night's flight, Walt had a cerebral infarction. I knew the symptoms were a stroke, so I immediately got the attendant and 2 passenger docs who concurred. We were over the Pacific, 8 hrs. from Bangkok, so the doctor and I asked the pilot to divert the plane to Tokyo, Japan, which was only 2 hrs to get him the drug TPA to stop permanent damage. They got permission to land that huge plane in Osaka because Tokyo had just had a #8 earthquake & the ground was unstable.

(Many Thai passengers stopped me on my way out of the plane and hugged me & bowed to Walt instead of being angry at the big delay we caused, which helped.)

An ambulance met us and a translator for Thai Air got off with me and stayed until we got to the hospital. CT scans and an MRI showed a lesion in the brain, but by then we were too late for TPA so he is getting Arthromatic IV for 24 hrs and they'll add edaravone to the drip line for about 6 days. He can't be moved until that is complete.

They brought me a cot so I could stay here with him and rest because the hotels are full with Tokyo residents fleeing the earthquake until tonight when I have room.

They hope I can take him back to Maine in one week. His left side is weak and drooping and his speech is slurred, and there will be some permanent damage, they say. He will need evaluation and rehabilitation upon our return.

Amy, please relay all this to his doctor Dr. Botler so he'll know we're going to need prompt care as soon as we get back.

I tell you all this because no one here in the entire hospital speaks English and I cannot make an international call until I get to a nearby hotel tonight. Rest assured that I will spend every waking hour in his room advocating for him, feeding him, and doing sign language to get good care. They said I have to leave at night. All devastating and scary!

With this Ellie relays the contact information about the hospital and hotel and signs the e-mail "Ellie/Mom. Very 'Lost in Translation.'"

Ellie leaves the Gateway Towers and makes her way across the Expressway to the hospital. She has not heard from anyone. Walt is resting and very glad to see her.

Meanwhile, Nirvana Expeditions has contacted Judith Meyers, who e-mails Robert. She tells Robert that his father had a stroke, and that Walt and Ellie were put off the plane in Osaka. Robert has no solid information about his father's status, but now he knows that the e-mail is not bogus, and the situation is serious.

≈

On March 13, 2011, the *Japan Times* reports the following:

Nothing could stop the terrifying waves that within seconds destroyed buildings and entire streets, reducing what used to be thriving communities into burning piles of shattered wood and rubble.

Paddy fields and farms that has provided livelihood for many were transformed into saltwater lagoons, the landscape unrecognizable from before the torrents of seawater thundered across the land.

More the 1,000 people were feared dead across the northeast.

The towering wall of water generated by the 8.8-magnitude earthquake pulverized the city of Sendai, where police reportedly said 200 to 300 bodies had been found on the coast.

At Fukushima Daiichi, the situation is disastrous. Radiation continues to pour out into the air and seawater, and over 200,000 people must be evacuated from a 10-mile radius of the plant. A municipal official in Fukushima Prefecture is quoted as saying, "More than ninety percent of the houses in the three coastal communities have been washed away by the tsunami. Looking from the fourth floor of town hall, I see no houses standing."

On Midway Atoll, the wave completely submerges the reef, killing more than 110,000 nesting seabirds. In Hawaii, it strikes private homes and resorts with estimates of tens of millions of dollars' damage. By Saturday, the tsunami has traveled across the Pacific and is striking the coasts of Oregon and California. Surges nearly eight feet high are sweeping into harbors. Cindy Henderson, emergency services manager in Crescent City, Oregon, about 340 mi north of San Francisco, is quoted as saying, "We have at least 35 boats that have been crushed. We have boats on top of other boats." In Curry County, Oregon, 3,600 feet of dock space, worth 7 million dollars, is destroyed.

Tokyo, unlike many towns north of it, is not deluged by the tsunami, but the earthquake paralyzes this futuristic city. The subway and other transit systems are shut down, and people are stuck in elevators all over the city. In fear, people head south for cities like Osaka. The hotels are filling up, and the tremendous influx of immigrants has barely started.

The Earthquake Research Institute finds that the quake has shifted the Earth's axis by 10 cm.

By now the world is starting to get the message. Red Sox pitcher Daisuke Matsuzaka tries to reach his grandmother. Oakland slugger Hideki Matsui prays for the victims. Pitcher Yoshinori Tateyama uses his fingers to draw a map and show Rangers teammates where the destruction is.

3

Family Mobilizes for Action

Saturday, 3/12/11

Ellie walks back to spend time with Walt. Later, she gathers their luggage, and one suitcase at a time, she starts back across the Expressway. This time she goes via the skywalk at the Gateway Towers, the top still swaying with aftershocks. In her room, she gets a call from Robert. Hearing his voice is an enormous relief.

"You speak English so well," she jokes.

By e-mail, Robert arranges a conference call on his work line for late evening for Ellie and himself in Asia and morning for the rest of the family in the States. Walt and Ellie's five children are all involved—daughters Maggie in Boston, Amy and Sandy in Maine, and son Brian in Texas. The emotional atmosphere surrounding this initial call is one of fear and mobilization. Everyone knows that Walt is in serious condition. Apparently, the country of Japan is, as well.

Sunday, 3/13/11

This morning, Walt again chokes on the miso soup. He has rattling in his chest, and Ellie is quite sure he is getting aspiration pneumonia. She raises this concern with the nurses, but is not understood.

At 7 a.m., Ellie joins the conference call with their five children and Dr. Joel Botler, Walt and Ellie's internist in Portland. This is the first time

Ellie has the opportunity to talk with the family, and she is most appreciative that Dr. Botler is there as well. She explains that Walt has had a cerebral infarction. He is paralyzed on the left side, with possible permanent damage. His speech is weak, and he tires easily. Ellie wonders when it will be safe for him to fly home. Again, she is quite concerned about the lack of a translator.

On the conference call, Ellie and the family define and divide up the jobs as follows: Robert, an expert on unearthing money laundering in Hong Kong, will be the point person in Asia. Maggie, an investment advisor, will assist Ellie with translation help in Osaka. Brian, a law professor, will deal with Blue Cross-Blue Shield on covering hospital bills in a foreign country. Amy, director of an agency concerned with global affairs, will coordinate providing rehabilitation in Maine and will assist Maggie in arranging the transportation back to the States by ISOS ambulance plane. Sandy, a gourmet chef and independent business owner, will ask her son, Alex, studying international relations in college, to contact the U.S. embassy in Japan to expedite Walt's leaving. Dr. Botler will research the effects of flying on brain trauma and the earliest Walt can fly. In the next call, each person will report what he or she has accomplished.

At noon on Sunday, Robert calls Ellie at the hospital and finds her increasingly worried about Walt's signs of pneumonia. She requests a chest X-ray, but the nurses tell her that the doctors are very resistant to requests from the family. Finally, however, the doctors consent. The X-ray is done, and pneumonia is confirmed.

In the meantime, Amy calls ISOS Global Travel, which assures the family that they will investigate the possibility of Walt flying back from Osaka on one of their planes. ISOS Global Travel is the medical insurance that Walt and Ellie have purchased for their trip to Bhutan. Their Bhutan trip leader was very insistent that they have this insurance because of the frequent need to medivac hikers out of Bhutan, where medical facilities are limited. No one foresaw that they would need such insurance in an urban area like Osaka, but the fact that they have it is a wonderful break for Walt and Ellie.

Maggie contacts Chinami Nishizawa, a friend of a Massachusetts friend. Chinami, living in Tokyo, has another best friend from high school who is currently in Osaka. Mrs. Shino Oka, Chinami's friend, is in no position to act as the hospital interpreter, but she can be of some comfort to Ellie as she searches for an English-competent individual to assist.

Shino arrives Sunday afternoon. She tells Ellie that both her father and her husband are doctors. Her father has Alzheimer's disease and is a patient at the same hospital. Ellie tells her about her efforts to get Walt treated for pneumonia, and Shino reacts with horror.

"You did not tell the doctor your husband has pneumonia?" she says.

"Yes, I did," Ellie replies.

Shino is shocked and explains that in Japan the doctor is god. Family never makes suggestions about patient care.

Ellie produces several pages written in Japanese that were given to her on arrival at the hospital, and Shino translates. It is a list of instructions to families of patients about providing clean linen for their family members in the hospital. Shino talks with the nurses and learns that the hospital has an interpreter Monday through Thursday from 10 a.m. to 3 p.m.

At 1:30 p.m. (Japan time) on Sunday, Robert and Maggie talk with representatives of ISOS, who promise to contact a colleague in Tokyo to obtain Walt's medical status. More information is needed before he can be moved. In a conference call, both Brian and Maggie state their intention to go to Japan, but Robert dissuades them. All agree that he is closest and will be the central point of contact in Asia until a clearer picture emerges in Osaka.

In the same conference call, Brian reviews his conversation with Anthem BC/BS. The representative in charge of Walt's benefits has stated that they do not cover claims out of the country. However, having read a great deal about Anthem's policies, Brian has done his homework, and he picks up the defensive quality in the woman's voice.

"What about the part of BC/BS called Card Blue?" he asks.

There is a long silence on the other end of the line. Finally the woman replies. "Yes, that will cover it," she answers reluctantly.

The Maine office of Blue Cross/ Blue Shield does not open until Monday, and in the meantime more information is needed about Walt and Ellie's policy. Brian suggests that Amy and Sandy go to their house to find the necessary documents.

At 3:18 p.m. Sunday, Robert talks again with the ISOS representative and learns there is no problem with the family communicating directly with the ISOS Tokyo office. Meanwhile, the hospital is deluged with calls from insurance representatives who are trying to reach Walt's treating doctors. However, the switchboards are overwhelmed due to persons seeking information about the earthquake, and so to reduce calls to the nursing station, Robert is told not to call the hospital. Only Ellie should speak with Dr. Ando, the ISOS doctor who will reach out to her.

At 8 p.m., Robert arranges another conference call with Ellie, Maggie, Amy, Brian, and Sandy. Ellie explains that she has met with Dr. Fukuyo, a young neurosurgeon. Despite Shino's warning, she tells the doctor that she believes Walt needs antibiotics. Dr. Fukuyo consents to only three days, but Ellie worries that this is not long enough. However, the doctor is firm. Again, he explains that the earliest Walt may leave the hospital is Friday.

The family learns the criteria for travel. Walt must be strong enough to sit up for two hours as a time, and a doctor or nurse will have to travel with him and ensure admission to Maine Medical Center. Maggie volunteers to contact Dr. Botler about hospital admission. Everyone agrees to stop calling the nursing station. In the meantime, Robert has made reservations to arrive in Osaka on Tuesday, and Brian reluctantly gives up his ticket. Everyone worries, because there is no guarantee that anyone can get in or out of Japan.

⁓

North of the city, millions of households experience interruptions of water, gas, and electricity. Tokyo Electric Power warns that there will be blackouts, not just in the zone of devastation, but in a much wider area due to a short supply of electricity from the damaged facilities.

In Iwate prefecture, the city of Rikuzenkata has been totally destroyed, with water reaching the third floor of city hall. Four trains running in a coastal area of Miyagi and Iwate are unaccounted for. In Fukushima, a commuter train lies strewn across a muddy landscape, while at Fukushima Daiichi, only the bottom half of Reactor 1 remains.

Search teams mobilize around the globe. The 66 members of the Japanese team hurry home from Christchurch, New Zealand, where they have been involved in similar work since an earthquake hit there two weeks ago. Washington sends 150 members, many of whom are quickly leaving their work in New Zealand as well. The South Korean team is already in Tokyo, and teams from Australia, New Zealand, and Singapore are on the way.

Tohoku region hospitals are overwhelmed. They are trying to help people who have lost their homes and need a safe place to stay. Power outages mean the hospitals have limited capacity. The makeshift hospital in Sendai is treating 400 patients, while the halls are filling with evacuees. Operating rooms were unusable due to a lack of running water.

On Monday afternoon, a classmate of Walt's sends Ellie an e-mail. He expresses sympathy and tells Ellie that he has distributed an e-mail to the theater group that Walt and Ellie attend. As he spreads the word, the message goes viral.

4

Subtle Clash of Cultures

Monday, 3/14/11

Despite his paralysis and problems with speech, the staff thinks Walt is a candidate for rehabilitation. On Monday, three therapists in white come to his room, and, with difficulty, they get him to the rehabilitation room.

A young man steps forward. Like the others, he is dressed in white and probably is a physical therapist. He acts deferentially, yet he is not rigid and has an open, friendly air. Walt likes his attitude. Unaware of the extent of his neurological injury, he intends to show them that he can get better.

The staff pulls Walt up to the parallel bars, and he guesses they want him to walk between them. The pneumonia has not yet impaired him, so he grips the bars and begins a measured passage. His right leg drags, but his left is working. The young man walks slowly beside him while the others watch, emitting sighs of pleasure as he takes each step. The bars are only twenty feet long, and when he reaches the end, the whole staff applauds. Unlike the nurses who only want him to lie perfectly still, these therapists seem delighted with his activity.

Walt would like to try the walk again, but apparently the therapists think that once is enough and take him back downstairs. Confused about why they are stopping, he thinks that perhaps tomorrow they will let him perform again. As they reach his room, his heart beats rapidly, and he feels hot. The nurses turn the bed back for him. This time it feels good to be within the white sheets.

Ellie is there, and he is happy. He loves to listen to her voice, which is so clear and confident. On the plane, he heard another voice—the doctor who helped him. The doctor, Jordan, was also very calm.

"I've talked with Dr. Botler," Ellie says. "He's going to arrange for you to be admitted to New England Rehabilitation Hospital."

Walt nods.

"We're going to get you back to Maine as soon as we can," she adds.

Rescue workers find the town of Minamisanriku completely destroyed, and 9,500 persons are missing. One thousand bodies have been recovered by Monday, March 14. Large parts of Kuji and the southern section of Ofunato are obliterated. Other demolished cities include Kamaishi, Miyako, Otsuchi, and Yamada in Iwate Prefecture, Namie and Soma in Fukushima Prefecture, and Shichigahama, Higashi-matsushima, Onagawa, Natori, Ishinomaki, and Kesennuma in Miyagi Prefecture. Near Oarai, a huge whirlpool is churning everything that floats into its center.

A later government study will reveal that only 58% of people in coastal areas in Iwate, Miyagi, and Fukushima prefecture heeded the tsunami warning and headed for high ground. Of those who evacuated, only 5% were caught in the tsunami. Of those who didn't, 49% were hit by the water.

Most of the 13,135 fatalities died by drowning; 62.2% of victims were age 60 or older, with 24% being in their 70s. Of the total victims, 14,308 drowned, 667 were crushed to death or died from internal injuries, and 145 perished from burns.

As a result of her original e-mail to the family going viral, e-mails to Ellie start arriving from the States. The outpouring of love is tremendous.

Tuesday, 3/15/11

As Ellie fears, three days of oral antibiotics are not enough, and an X-ray of Walt's chest shows increasing consolidation in his lungs. He does not want to get out of bed. At Ellie's request, the doctor, still reluctant, puts him on nasal oxygen and gives him a more potent intravenous antibiotic. Since he cannot eat, the doctor orders an IV drip of D5W. From now until the very last day, the doctor, out of shame, will not look Ellie in the eyes. His head is always lowered.

Robert arrives with Sin Wah, his partner, and immediately begins to help Ellie with the many tasks at the hospital. Brian handles the BC/BS Card Blue request, while Amy coordinates future stateside rehabilitation with Dr. Botler. Sandy's son, Alex, checks with the U.S. embassy in Japan to determine if any action is necessary to expedite Walt's departure.

Walt is glad to see Robert and tries to communicate his pleasure. Then Ellie and Robert try to figure out how much the hospital bill will be and how they will pay in order not to impede Walt's release from the hospital. Meanwhile, the disaster is worsening, and the hospital is overflowing with victims of the earthquake and tsunami. Word is that many more are on the way.

In a press conference, a Tokyo water purification manager states that twenty-three wards of Tokyo and some places in the city of Tama have radiation-contaminated tap water. High radiation has been detected in soil about 40 km from Fukushima Daiichi, where radioactive vapor is escaping from a broken containment vessel.

Wednesday, 3/16/11

All around him, Walt feels activity, but Ellie always has time for him. He loves the sound of her voice. Robert and the rest of the family are trying to figure out if their credit cards carry enough limit to pay the hospital bill. If Walt stays through the week, that bill could top $20,000.

Workers at Fukushima Daiichi struggle to control the radiation. They can only work for short intervals due to serious health implications.

Helicopters airlift seawater and drop it over the top of reactors, but this activity has not decreased the temperature in the pools with spent fuel rods, where it remains very high. The helicopters must hover motionless for some time to dump the water over the reactors, and this maneuver is extremely dangerous. Consequently, crews are erecting water cannons to spell the helicopters.

In the northern provinces, the search for bodies goes on. The waters of the tsunami have receded, and the wreckage of thousands of homes and businesses lies in the mud. In boots, flip-flops, or even bare feet, rescue workers pull apart fractured piles of lumber in an effort to find those who did not survive. Bodies are respectfully stored in large open spaces, and families, looking for their loved ones, stream though these acres of the dead. The 40-foot tsunami walls that had previously seemed such good preparation now lie breached or collapsed. More than 300 hospitals are damaged, with 11 fully shut down.

E-mail letters from well-wishers continue to flood in. Ellie is very moved and sends a reply:

> Dear Friends,
> Finally a quiet moment to respond to all the messages of love and support from so many of you. I am so very grateful for your e-mails (and for e-mail itself!). For those of you who don't know what happened last Friday when we were flying nonstop from Los Angeles to Bangkok, I'm just taking a shortcut by putting a copy of my first e-mail to our children at the end of this note.
> The first two days were very rough since no one spoke English and it took a while for me to reach our family, but a translator finally arrived and I didn't feel so alone. Walt is showing marked improvement with stroke symptoms, but has developed pneumonia. Our 5 children and their spouses have been absolutely amazing, working like an efficient, well-oiled machine to help us through this and to get home ASAP because the situation here in Japan is a true disaster, and getting worse

every day. We must get out of the country as soon as it's safe for Walt to travel because sick people are now pouring into Osaka and the hospital from Tokyo and north.

Rob, in Hong Kong, Maggie in Mass., Amy and Sandy in Maine, Brian in Texas, and I have talked daily on a conference phone line that Rob can access through his work. They even patched in [Walt's] doctor in Maine! Working beautifully together, they have arranged through International SOS, to have a small Leer jet ambulance plane that is returning to the U.S. from Singapore, pick us up on Sunday and take the two of us to Portland. We'll be stopping a couple of times to refuel. In the meantime, Rob and his partner flew here 2 days ago to help his dad and to see us get on the SOS plane home. It is so good to have company. Walt and I are more grateful for our children than I can express.

And, to all of you good friends who are there for us, thank you, thank you! Walt said your thoughts and prayers give him hope.

Much love,
Ellie

Friday, 3/18/11, morning

The interpreter has arranged a meeting with hospital administrators to discuss the bill. Ellie needs to know whether the sum can be covered by credit cards, since she is not carrying much cash with her. She and Robert meet the interpreter at the hospital, and she escorts them to a meeting room. As she enters, she bows deferentially to the six men in white shirts, dark ties, and black suits who are sitting in a semicircle of chairs. The men do not smile, and the interpreter tells Ellie and Robert that they should take their seats opposite them. The interpreter takes a seat to their right.

The interpreter and the men talk, and she does not translate what they discuss. There is an awkward silence, and Ellie and Robert shift in their chairs. Finally Ellie asks about the cost of the hospitalization, and the interpreter translates. However, the expression on the men's faces remains stern. As the meeting progresses, both Ellie and Robert sense that they are missing something. Ellie is not sure the interpreter has understood her, but Robert has other ideas.

"I think I know what's wrong," he says. "They think we're trying to get out of paying the bill."

"Do they think we're trying not to pay the bill?" Ellie asks the interpreter, "because we *are* trying to pay!"

The interpreter translates Ellie's statement, and six faces relax with expressions of relief.

"Ahh, ho," the six men say in unison.

Ellie and Robert are flabbergasted, but contain themselves. The meeting ends well.

5

Escape

Friday, 3/18/11, afternoon

Days and nights have merged for Walt, and Friday is a long time coming. By Tuesday, his pneumonia had gotten worse, and he was very tired. The IV antibiotic, although potent, has given him a rash. However, Ellie has been with him. She handles problems with cheeriness and confidence, and he loves to listen to her.

In mid-afternoon on Friday, Ellie and Walt are in his room when the head doctor appears. He is a handsome man in his early fifties with a smattering of English from one month's study in Philadelphia. Proud of his English and wanting to be seen as a person who is sophisticated about the West, he chats away for a few minutes about experiences in the States. Ellie patiently responds, knowing that the power of the decision about whether they can go home is in his hands. Finally, he announces that the hospital is getting dangerous with all the sick and injured patients coming in from the north, and he has decided to approve Walt's discharge for tomorrow morning. After more small talk, he goes.

Ellie is enormously relieved. Although the head doctor doesn't reveal it, she knows that ISOS initiated contact with him. In fact, she and the family have worked closely with ISOS since Monday, and an ISOS plane, originating in Australia and currently in Shanghai, will come to Osaka on Sunday morning and to take them home. ISOS has told her they will do all the negotiating with the doctor, because they know the diplomacy necessary in Japan to save face in all circumstances.

Today, March 18th, is Ellie's birthday, and she returns to her hotel room to find a beautiful bouquet of flowers sent by Walt's sister, Jane, his niece, Patricia, and his mother, Polly. In addition, Robert and Sin Wah take her to dinner, and the three of them walk around Osaka until they find an appealing restaurant.

Saturday, 3/19/11

Reports are coming in from Antarctica confirming that the tsunami has reached that distant point 8,100 miles away and broken icebergs off the Sulzberger Ice Shelf. The biggest iceberg created is about the area of Manhattan and is 260 feet thick.

Following the earthquake at Ichihara, Chiba Prefecture, to the east of Tokyo, the Cosmo Oil refinery catches fire, and 220,000 barrels of oil are still burning. Radioactive iodine is found in the tap water in Fukushima, Tochigi, Gunma, Tokyo, Chiba, Saitama, and Niigata. Radioactive cesium is found in the taps of Fukushima, Tochigi, and Gunma. This area of radioactivity is considerably wider than expected.

Ellie tries to purchase her yogurt, which has been her main food for days, and finds it has been pulled from the shelf due to the danger of radioactivity.

In the first days after the quake, the disrupted train and bus service causes 20,000 stranded visitors to spend a sleepless night inside Tokyo Disneyland, but now, a week later, transportation in Osaka has returned to normal. However, many sections of Tohoku Expressway serving northern Japan remain damaged, and it will not reopen until the 24th of March, six days from now. The Tohoku Shinkansen train line is still unusable, and workmen are trying to repair the 1,100 sections of the line suffering from collapsed roofs and bent power pylons.

Ellie sits with Walt and tells him what will happen when they get home. "I think you'll be admitted to New England Rehabilitation

Hospital," she says. "It's possible you may be admitted to Maine Medical first. Dr. Botler has arranged that depending on your condition."

Walt nods. He's so happy to be going home.

Sunday, 3/20/11

In Osaka, cellular and landline phone service is being restored, but it is still down in the affected area of the northern coast. Immediately after the earthquake, cellular communication across much of Japan was jammed due to a surge of network activity, and only a few websites were initially reachable. Wi-Fi hot spot providers stepped in and provided free access to their networks.

Two days from now, there will still be more than one million households without water, and the problem with radioactivity will continue to grow. As late as July, four months after the quake, elevated levels of radioactivity will still be found in beef on sale in the Tokyo market.

At 9:00 Sunday morning, Ellie and Robert stand beside Walt's bed as they wait for the Swiss team from ISOS. At the appointed time, two women and two men appear. They are very professional, with the women in dark gray suits, gray stockings, and gray hats and the men in white shirts and dark gray suits. They all carry briefcases.

"It is all taken care of," one of them says.

The doctor and staff enter with a wheelchair. The ISOS representatives speak with Walt's doctor.

"You will ride in the ambulance and go aboard the plane to pronounce that your patient is fit to go," they say to the doctor.

The doctor is very pleased with this assignment, and he raises his eyes for the first time since his discussion with Ellie about pneumonia.

"Mrs. Christie, you will ride with your husband in the ambulance," the ISOS representatives say.

Ellie nods.

"And Mr. Christie," they say to Robert, "you will say goodbye to your parents at the door of the hospital."

Robert and Sin Wah say goodbye to Walt as he is getting into the wheelchair.

One of the staff pushes Walt out to a waiting ambulance. The doctor and Ellie get in, and the ambulance starts on its way through the same gray city that Walt and Ellie flew into ten days before. The Leer jet sits idling on the tarmac, and the three pilots are waiting outside the plane. They introduce themselves, and then the ambulance staff takes Walt into the plane where a pleasant-looking Asian physician and an Australian nurse direct them to put him on a chest-high stretcher. The Japanese doctor examines Walt and finds him fit to travel. Then he bows and steps off the plane.

The small jet is comfortably appointed with the stretcher-bed for Walt, a comfortable chair for Ellie, and a couch in the rear to rest on. In the cockpit are two seats for the pilots on duty and a comfortable seat for the third pilot not on duty. The pilots are friendly and very professional.

The lead pilot explains that it will be a twenty-hour trip from Japan to Portland, Maine. Along the way there will be three fueling stops— Petropavlosk, Siberia; Anchorage, Alaska; and Billings, Montana. The first stop is the base in the former Soviet Union where in 1983 missiles were launched against Korean Air Lines flight 007, killing all 269 passengers and crew.

The doors close and the crew prepares for takeoff, but the plane is put on hold when another plane from China arrives with a very high-level government delegation to meet with Japanese officials. On the ISOS plane, they watch out the windows as eight or ten Chinese men in dark suits walk in a line toward a row of Japanese men in black suits, who walk in unison to shake hands and bow. When they clear the field, the ISOS plane is approved for the takeoff. In less than a minute, the plane is airborne and headed out of Japan.

As the plane leaves, the Japanese are picking up the pieces after the earthquake and tsunami. On the first day, they lost 230,000 cars and trucks. Military losses included 18 jets of the Japan Self-Defense Force when Matsushima Air Field was struck by the tsunami. Twelve of these aircraft must be scrapped, while the remaining six are slated for repair at a cost of one billion dollars each. At the 2nd Regional Headquarters of the Japan Coast Guard in Shiogama, Miyagi, two patrol boats were swept away.

Petropavlovsk, the first stop, 1,777 miles from Osaka, is located on Siberia's Kamchatka Peninsula and carries the distinction of being the second largest city in the world unreachable by road. The city is surrounded by high, snow-capped volcanoes that block the view of the horizon. In March, the average high temperature is −3 degrees. Petropavlovsk is approximately due north of Japan.

The plane lands at a broad, flat military base. When it comes to a halt, there is a noticeable silence in the cabin. The pilots are very tense. The doctor and the nurse are quiet and watchful. Ellie peers through the glass and sees three or four men in hazmat suits moving around the plane with wands. In the cabin, the tension is palpable, and Ellie can hear a pilot in the cockpit talking with ground control. His manner is very halting. Meanwhile, the men move their wands over all surfaces of the airplane.

"What's going on?" Ellie whispers to the doctor.

In a low voice he replies. "They are checking us for radiation," he says. "If the Geiger counters go off due to radiation on the hull, we go back to Japan.

"And," he continues, "none of us really want that."

The men in hazmat suits continue to wand the outside of the plane, and then the door opens, and one of them pokes his wand inside. Ellie and the doctor watch him. After about a minute, he withdraws. The door shuts, and the pilots are visibly relieved.

"We're all gassed up, and we can go," one pilot says.

Lightness and relief fill the plane as it takes off toward Anchorage.

Anchorage, Alaska's largest city, is 2,409 miles from Petropavlovsk. Well situated to refuel planes, it is within nine and a half hours of 90% of the industrialized world. Walt sleeps on the stretcher, sedated by the good judgment of the Asian doctor, who, like the crew, projects calm and professionalism. Whichever pilot is not on duty prepares the hot meals, and Ellie feels well cared for. The plane lands in Anchorage, and the pilot can barely contain himself.

"Ladies," he says, "we are on U.S. soil, and I would like you to get off the plane, use the loo, and have a cup of coffee—but as you get off, I want you to bend down and kiss this USA soil!"

Ellie and the nurse get out of the plane, while someone stays with Walt. Lights appear brighter here. The Muzak is playing American songs. It is the first sign of homecoming.

Billings, Montana, is 1,961 miles from Anchorage, and the airfield is a small strip outside the city. Billings is smaller that Petropavlovsk and Anchorage, but it is still the largest city in Montana. Billings is susceptible to extreme weather, and nine months earlier, residents experienced the Father's Day tornado that brought golf-ball-sized hail, dangerous cloud-to-ground lightning, and heavy winds. Today, however, the weather is nice, and Ellie, the nurse, the doctor, and the pilots go inside a small hangar. Then, after a few minutes, they re-board the plane for Portland, Maine, 1,867 miles from Billings.

At this point, the earthquake and tsunami begin to fade a little from Walt and Ellie's minds. They are concerned with only one thing—getting Walt well again. They leave behind them a major humanitarian and economic crisis. The tsunami results in over 340,000 displaced people in the Tohoku region, and shortages of food, water, shelter, medicine, and fuel for survivors.

The aftermath of the twin disasters also leaves Japan's coastal cities and towns with nearly 25 million tons of debris. In Ishinomaki alone, there are 17 trash collection sites 200 yards long and at least 15 feet high. An official in the city's government trash disposal department estimates that it will take three years to empty these sites.

6

Rehabilitation, Smallness of the World

The pilot announces they are putting down in Portland, and Ellie takes a moment to thank the doctor and nurse. An ambulance is idling to take Walt to New England Rehabilitation Hospital, where his room is waiting. Walt is disoriented and mistakenly believes that the hospital is located on Congress Street, below Maine Medical Center.

When they arrive, Ellie speaks with the admitting staff while Walt is taken to his room. Dr. Botler has prepared the admission, so the process moves swiftly and easily. Amy is there to greet them, and she sends an e-mail to the rest of the family stating that Ellie and Walt have arrived. They are all right, she says, although both look tired and thin.

After spending time with Walt, Ellie goes to her temporary residence at Amy's house. David, Amy's husband, understands her need for a place to stay close to the hospital, and he makes a pied-à-terre on the third floor. He and Amy also go to Ellie and Walt's house in Freeport to get Ellie some clothes and her computer. Meanwhile, Sandy and Chris offer to keep Abby, Walt and Ellie's dog, until he comes home.

Walt lies awake most of the night. He slept very little in Osaka, and the pattern continues. His mind is focused on one thing—getting better. To him, it is inconceivable that he will *not* get better. He just has to work on it, no matter how hard.

Morning comes, and the dietary staff wheels him into the dining room. The supervisor of the dining room is also a speech therapist, and as he brings trays around, he carefully watches each patient eat. Walt is seated in a chair next to a small table. The director brings him a cube of a nondescript, gelatinous substance and a small cup of juice. He gestures for Walt to begin eating. It has been about six days since Walt has eaten any food, and he looks around the room where other patients are eating. Some have generous offerings of eggs, pancakes, and coffee, while others have only the cubes of whatever-it-is like his.

His right hand is very weak, but he picks up his spoon. He ladles a mouthful of the substance into his mouth and immediately begins to cough. The supervisor watches carefully as Walt puts down the spoon and coughs. Then he tries again and manages to get two mouthfuls down before coughing again.

"You'll get this," the supervisor says. "Keep working at it."

Walt does continue and gets through the whole cube and the glass of juice. It requires enormous concentration, and when he lifts his head up and looks around for other patients, they have finished their breakfasts and returned to their rooms. He is the only one still in the dining room.

"At noon, you will get a pork cube," the supervisor says. "That was chicken."

Then an orderly wheels him back to his room. It has taken all of his energy just to eat, but he keeps working on eating, since there is really nothing else he can do. The three sessions per day in the dining room prove to be the most exhausting of his rehabilitation exercises, but every day he makes a little progress.

Ellie and Dr. Kasmi are waiting in his room. Dr. Kasmi had polio as a child, and now he cares for neurologically impaired people with his legs in two metal braces. He has a nice manner, and he examines Walt thoroughly. He tells Walt that he has arranged a roommate, a former Navy pilot whom he thinks Walt will enjoy.

When Dr. Kasmi has gone, Ellie explains how David and Amy have made her a pied-à-terre, how Abby, the dog, is comfortably situated with Sandy and Chris, and how India, the cat, can stay at the kennel in

Northport. She is about to tell him about the many e-mails they have received, but it's time for his occupational therapy.

The white board attached to the wall reads:

Occupational therapy—9:15 a.m.
Speech therapy—10:00 a.m.
Ambulation—11:00 a.m.
Speech therapy—1:15 p.m.
Occupational therapy—2:30

The day is laid out for Walt. His new roommate, who had a stroke during cardiac surgery, has a different schedule, but also very full.

Ellie leaves to collect their mail from the post office while Walt goes to occupational therapy. The therapist tosses an inflated ball to him, and Walt catches it. Although slow, his reflexes are good, and she devises a more complicated task. She takes Walt out in the hall and tosses a tennis ball toward him. The distance he must throw is greater than before, and she carefully observes his weakness on the right. Since he does pretty well, she gives him a tennis ball and asks him to throw it to her. Then she returns the throw and watches how he catches the ball. With this exercise, he does not do as well.

In occupational therapy, the tasks get harder. The therapist includes the task of throwing the ball while walking and then adds balancing on a teeter board and tossing the ball. When Walt returns to his room, he is very tired, and the fatigue increases each day. However, he is doing better and better.

It is time for speech therapy. This discipline appeals to Walt, because it promises to work on "where the lesion is." Because he is a physician with an interest in neurology, finding the lesion is of paramount importance to him. He believes that if he understands the portion of the brain that is impaired, he can correct it. It is just a matter of concentrating on the neurological pathways and learning to reuse them. His right-sided paralysis is a crude indicator, but with his speech, he believes that he will have a more refined sense of where the disorder-producing lesion lies.

The speech therapist takes him to a room with several machines. She asks him to repeat a number of words that appear on the screen of one machine. His speech is very weak, but Walt feels a pattern emerging in his mispronunciation, which is trying to tell him about the lesion. The twice-daily speech therapy continues to interest him very much, particularly the day when the director of speech therapy gives him a session.

Walt has seen a lot of the director, since he also supervises the dining room. Now he works with Walt with a machine that isolates problems with consonants. Walt has particular problems with some consonants, and the director teaches him that if he focuses more on the vowels that come before the consonants, he will find that the consonants are not as hard to pronounce. Walt does this and is amazed.

He returns to his room after speech therapy and is even more tired. However, a nurse is there, and she is ready to walk him. They go up and down the hall, and if that is not enough, they go off the ward and down a long parallel corridor. Walt is exhausted, but he says nothing. Finally, the nurse brings him to his room. With relief, he sinks into his bed. His roommate, the Navy pilot, blind from the stroke during heart surgery, says a cheery hello. Walt can barely muster a reply.

He has just settled into the bed when the dietary staff comes in.

"Time for your lunch," they say.

Until he is capable of walking freely, the staff takes him in a wheelchair. Frankly, he is so tired that he welcomes that wheelchair. He has an enormous fatigue that will be troublesome for many months to come. This fatigue is not typical tiredness, but comes from the reworking that the post-stroke nervous system does. The intact cells of the damaged brain send out new connections to other cells, and the brain reorganizes itself. If there are enough intact cells and enough new connections, the brain functions almost as well as before, although somewhat slower in function. In the meantime, he gets very tired around 1 p.m. every day.

In mid-afternoon Ellie returns, and he is very glad to see her. Family comes to visit, and Ellie helps Walt talk with them. She fields questions and offers support. Several days into the rehabilitation, she tells him a story. It involves India, their cat, a two-hour trip to Northport to pick him up at a kennel, and a flat tire when she neared her pied-à-terre on return.

The story that Ellie tells is about getting the flat tire a couple of miles from Amy's, and instead of calling from the busy road, she drives home on the tire. Inside, she greets Amy and the children, takes off her coat and boots, and calmly calls AAA, acting as though nothing has happened. From Ellie's perspective, nothing much *has* happened, but Amy sees it differently.

"That's not normal!" Amy says. "You act as if nothing has happened. Walt's in the hospital, you've just driven up the coast and back, and you had a flat tire, yet you're acting like its nothing at all."

Ellie turns to her. "It doesn't *seem* like anything much," she says. "I had a flat tire."

She realizes that her perspective has really altered after dealing with the enormous events of the past few weeks, and these daily annoyances don't seem like much to handle.

As Walt is finishing his inpatient rehabilitation, his roommate tells him about an amazing coincidence. He has received an e-mail from a friend, another former Navy pilot who now flies for Delta. The friend was piloting a plane that was right behind Walt's plane as he tried to land in Tokyo. His friend sent out an e-mail to other pilots. Someone put it on the Internet, and it went viral. Walt is amazed that his roommate in Maine should have a friend in the plane just behind him in Osaka. In some ways, he thinks, it is a very small world.

Walt is ready to go home and get some rest. The rehabilitation has moved him forward, but he is exhausted. The rehab staff emphasizes the homework that he must do. Dr. Kasmi wishes him well and urges him to keep working. A social worker in charge of discharge planning connects him to the outpatient rehabilitation staff. Finally, fully prepared for the next step, Walt and Ellie go to their home in Freeport, because outpatient therapy will begin immediately.

In the time since Walt and Ellie left Japan, five million tons of debris have dispersed in the ocean around the Japanese islands. About 70% of this sinks soon after drifting from shore, but a portion of the smaller debris drifts north and east of the Hawaiian archipelago. No one can predict the course of the larger debris as it floats out into the Pacific.

7

Facing Reality, Vastness of the World

Walt and Ellie get to their home in Freeport, and she helps him into bed. Then she goes downstairs and surveys the place for safety. With great effort, Walt can get upstairs, but he has to pick up his weak right leg and shift his weight to his left. He can grasp most things with his right hand, but he cannot perform finer movements. His voice is very weak, and he cannot pronounce some words. He can only eat by sitting up very straight, thoroughly chewing his food, and swallowing slowly. Mostly, he maneuvers from the bed upstairs to a chair or sofa downstairs. Eventually, with extra effort, he can make it to a sofa in the basement where their TV is situated.

At New England Rehabilitation Hospital, a full outpatient schedule awaits them—occupational and speech therapy two or three times a week. Since it is a half hour both ways, Ellie tries to minimize their driving, but sometimes the therapists just cannot organize appointments on the same day. Walt willingly goes to each therapy session, but he is tired. At times it feels like too much to open his eyes and speak. After the sessions, he is glad to be going home to bed.

The outpatient occupational therapy is an extension of what he did as an inpatient. No longer is he asked to bounce or catch a ball; instead, he must perform small actions of a repetitive nature and then more complicated tasks that require eye-hand coordination. One of these exercises involves the driving board. It is a large flat surface with lights that go on and off in a random fashion. Walt must watch carefully for each light to illuminate and quickly try to turn it off. The board measures his reaction time, and it is directly relevant to his ability to drive. Walt works very hard on this, because the loss of permission to drive would be an enormous blow for him.

In addition to therapy sessions, the occupational therapist gives him homework, so Walt and Ellie ask their grandchildren to bring him puzzles. At first, the large-piece floor puzzles supplied by Bennett, age 5, are enough of a challenge, but very soon he is ready more for complicated types supplied by Sophie and Henry, age 8. Then he pits his brain against Charlie's puzzles and ends with Satchel's selection of 1,000-piece types.

Steve, Walt's speech therapist, has identified ways to help strengthen his voice. He encourages him to practice a series of words at a certain pitch. To Walt, it feels like yelling, but Steve assures him that this is ordinary volume. Walt discovers things about the way he talked before the stroke that are a problem now. For example, he finds that he starts to talk before he has formulated his words. Also, he realizes that when he speaks, he experiences his speech as muffled, yet when he uses a tape recorder to record it, his speech sounds normal. Steve is puzzled by this, but again reassures Walt that he is all right.

Walt and Ellie are deeply involved in the rehabilitation process when their landlady suddenly comes for a visit. She announces that she intends to sell the property, and since they are such good renters, she wants to offer them a chance to buy the house. Although it is a nice house, they conclude that it is too expensive, so in the midst of stroke and rehabilitation they have to move.

The crisis in Japan continues. In the hard-hit prefectures, acres of debris clog the streets of what once were towns. All of the water has not receded, and pools of mud and water dot the landscape. The resettlement has barely begun, and thousands are living in poorly ventilated barren buildings. Food is scarce, and the ability to stay healthy is marginal. Among the elderly, the rate of pneumonia is five times higher than usual. Because the Japanese respect calm and restraint, talk of legal action is at a minimum, but with deceased parents, many people will have a hard time establishing ownership of their damaged properties. Anguished families still search the rivers for their loved ones, but the chance of finding bodies now is slim.

Walt is not able to contribute much energy to their move, so Ellie starts packing the entire house, while Alex, who has come home from college, helps Ellie get their finances online. He reorganizes Walt's and Ellie's passwords and visits the accountant with Ellie to help prepare taxes for the next year. Then he helps Ellie pack for the movers, along with Ellie's dear friend, Judith Moll, who comes from Portland for long days of work.

Ellie arranges for their furniture to go into storage as they go to their summer place at Sebasco, a lovely old ocean cottage that Ellie's parents left to her. Walt really can do very little, so Alex and Nick launch the boat for him, and Nick mows the lawn. Walt is unhappy that the fatigue robs him of his energy, but he accepts it for the short run. In the meantime, he misses their dog, Abby, and asks for her to come back.

Since the first hours of his stroke, Walt has felt a unity of his mind in which everything is whole. In some way, he has always been like this, but not to this degree. The continual feeling of wholeness overcomes any brokenness he might feel and allows him to go on.

Unfortunately, he does not have enough feedback to show him that he cannot go back to work, and Ellie pleads with him not to. However, he stubbornly hangs on. In his mind, he is getting better, and it seems like his job as a psychiatric consultant for the retirement system is doable. The workplace will go a bit easy on me, he theorizes. I'll probably get three or four cases where I have primary responsibility for judging disability.

Two weeks go by, and a large box arrives from the retirement system. In it are the 11 cases for which he has primary responsibility. He groans at the number, but takes a deep breath and starts in. There are thousands of pages of medical records to review, and since he can't write longhand to make notes, he copies the pertinent pages on a copier. This proves to be extremely time-consuming, but unless he organizes the pages into a conclusion, he loses his train of thought. His difficulty with organization proves a problem, because the principal case has already been reviewed by two psychiatrists who could not agree. I'll form my own opinion, he thinks, and then I will present it to the medical board.

The day arrives, and he gets a ride with another physician board member. On the way to Augusta, he recounts the details of his stroke. The doctor asks him if he is ready for the board, and he answers yes. He walks in to find that the two psychiatrists who reviewed the case are both seated in the room. He has never been to a board where two psychiatrists have been in attendance. Now, including him, there are three. Perhaps the other two will help me if I do not have all the facts, he thinks.

Walt is introduced to the second psychiatrist, who got his training in the military. Walt then starts by reading his report on this service-connected case. The two psychiatrists sit stony-faced and silent. It becomes clear that everyone but Walt knows facts about the case not contained in the record. He is acutely aware that since the stroke he lacks the ability to speak off the cuff, and his report is all he has. He can tell from looking at the faces in the room that it is not enough.

"What opinions do *you* have?" Walt asks the psychiatrist he knows. However, the military psychiatrist intrudes.

"In the military, we have a name for these cases," he says, and Walt can tell that not only is he going to disagree with him, but he's going to demonstrate that his military training in service-connected disabilities is better that Walt's.

Walt listens to the new psychiatrist discuss the case, and he can tell that he is pleasing the retirement staff. All right, he thinks, there is nothing to do but swallow my pride and move on. With that, he goes to the second case, which goes more smoothly.

On his way back home, he asks the physician driving him about the new psychiatrist. The doctor explains that he was hired because the staff wanted three psychiatrists instead of two for reasons like his stroke. Walt thinks about this situation and the board's lack of empathy for him.

He thinks about the way the second psychiatrist played up his military background and about the other information that Walt himself did not receive. If he had an intact brain, he would view the situation as a challenge, but if he were forced to go to court with the case and his current brain, he might lose. By the time he reaches home, it is clear what he should do: retire.

His family is relieved. Ellie has been begging him to retire. Now he, too, sees that it makes eminent sense, and he settles down to enjoy the summer. His grandsons continue to help him by mowing the lawn, and someone always goes with him to drive the boat.

As the summer progresses, he concentrates on enjoying himself. Two neighbors appear at his door bearing mystery novels. Prior to the stroke, Walt had been reading P.D. James and Elizabeth George, two fine practitioners of mystery writing. The neighbors bring lots of books. They are fascinating, and he can't put them down. He likes the music-loving detective of Peter Robinson's books, but it is Henning Mankill's Swedish stories, with plots relying on international intrigue, that really capture him. Happily, he reads and reads.

He and Ellie talk about psychological testing. He had given his initial history to the psychologist in the spring, and Ellie feels that he should complete the testing to get a picture of what is wrong. Walt agrees and makes his appointment for the fall, when he will resume his therapy.

On September 12th and 14th, he undergoes the testing at NERH. Dr. Philip Morse is the interpreter. An experienced psychologist administers the tests. She does not slow down or stop, and Walt is very tired by the second day. She pools her raw data and delivers the results to Dr. Morse. His findings are as follows:

First and foremost, difficulties with attention and concentration are particularly noticeable…In addition, the problems with attention also impact his performance on measures of complex problem solving/executive functioning…Either he gets overloaded by too much material to process at once or has not paid adequate attention to the material in order to remember it…

Walt listens to the results of the testing and is truly glad he retired. He obviously underestimated the damage done by the stroke. He reads the testing over several times. His testing is valid, and his deficit is clear. Meanwhile, his friends are telling him how well he is doing. They describe him as "a miracle." One friend says, "He gives us hope."

Walt is surprised by his friends' enthusiasm about his recovery, and he speaks to Ellie about it.

"It's true," she says. "Look at how well you're doing."

Walt shakes his head. He cannot think of doing otherwise.

≈

In September 2011, a Russian ship finds debris floating northwest of Midway Atoll. The Russians have been warned that they might encounter the results of the tsunami, but when they discover a 20-foot fishing boat, their alarm about radioactivity grows. They test the hull with a Geiger counter and are relieved to find no radioactivity.

≈

Ellie looks for housing, and as fall approaches, one of Sandy's friends offers a wonderful little house next to her place on Ram Island Farm. Thirty-nine years before, during psychiatric residency, when he was last at Ram Island, Walt thought it would be nice to live there. A large piece of the coast in Cape Elizabeth, it offers a long beach and magnificent houses that face the ocean. Sandy's friend offers the place, furnished and at a decent rate, and Walt and Ellie move in.

Ram Island is beautiful. Walt and Ellie enjoy walking Abby, and the owners of the property are most kind to them. Sadly, Abby gets diagnosed with cancer, and in spite of chemotherapy, a month later she dies.

Ram Island is idyllic, but Walt and Ellie need to find a place in Portland so as not to be on the road so much. One day, as they are driving along the Eastern Promenade, they see a For Rent sign. Ellie has always dreamed of living there.

"Let's check it out," Walt says.

When they get back to Ram Island, they call and learn it is a first-floor, one-bedroom apartment that has just been vacated. Although it is very small, it will give them the window on Portland they have been looking for. The Ram Island family is very obliging, and in January 2012, Walt and Ellie move to the Eastern Prom.

One of the items Walt brings with him to the apartment is a box that he has carried for thirty years. In it is an unfinished novel, started in earnest for an MFA in Writing but given up because it was too hard to write while practicing psychiatry full-time. The book is about Maine Indians in the first part of the seventeenth century. After a terrible winter with the threat of starvation, the hero and his fiancée, both Pegwakets from Kezar Lake, come to the shore, but then the tribe is massacred. The hero survives, but his fiancée is carried off. Both believe that they are the only survivors, and thus they establish full lives in the Anasagunticook and Wawenock tribes. Each is married, and the hero has children before discovering that they both survived.

The box contains a number of versions of Walt's opening chapters, each one started with a different teacher in the MFA course. I have nothing to lose, Walt thinks. I'll start the book again.

On March 11, 2012, Walt watches the news on the first anniversary of the earthquake and tsunami, and the news video is replaying the tsunami wave breaching the walls, filling the town, and destroying huge buildings. He has never seen any of the footage on the tsunami and is amazed at its power.

"Ellie," he calls, "you've got to come here and see this!"

Ellie, who has lived the earthquake and tsunami and seen Japanese TV replaying it over and over, can only react with dismay at what Walt does not know.

"No-o-o!!" she says emphatically, but then she quietly adds, "I've seen it."

-8-

Branching out

One year after the earthquake and tsunami, Japan grapples with the human, economic, and political costs. The death toll is now estimated at 16,000, but nearly 3,300 remain unaccounted for. Koyu Morishita, who owns a destroyed home and family-run fish factory in the port of Ofunato, still searches for his father, Tokusaburo, but the old man's body has not been found. At exactly 2:46 p.m. on March 11, 2012, everyone in Ofunato observes a moment of silence. The "bell of hope" tolls, and mourners set out to sea to release their lanterns.

In the winter of 2011–2012, Ellie receives an amazingly generous invitation from Judith Meyers to use her and Michael's condominium in San Francisco. With Judith's activities in Tibetan countries, Ellie thinks about her own time there. She remembers Nepal and the breathtaking hike through the Dhampus trek from Kathmandu and the Annapurna Sanctuary trek from Pokara. After acclimating at 7,000 feet, she and Ginny went on to Tibet, where they visited the Potala Palace, ancestral home of the Dalai Lama. Leaving Lhasa, they hiked through the high desert at 13,000 feet and across a glacier-fed lake that nomads crossed in yak-skin boats, to the remote Samye monastery. The thrill of being on that high plateau has never left her.

Walt, in the meantime, has found a program in Portland that interests him greatly. Greater Portland Landmarks facilitates a "PHD"—Portland Historical Docents—program, a coordinated effort by eight local historical sites to train new docents. The program offers general historical lectures and a site visit to each facility. Docent work requires that a person have command of the pertinent historical information and be able to speak clearly. Walt does know whether he can do either, but he wants to find out.

The Bhutan trip for Ellie was intended to start a new chapter with the Tibetans. Now that Walt has had the stroke, she must put those dreams on the shelf—permanently. San Francisco, on the other hand, is a place they both love—the city on seven hills with the Marin County landscape to the north and Monterey and Big Sur to the south. She knows that Walt would enjoy the trip if he is fit enough to go.

Walt listens as she recounts the offer of the condominium. It is an extraordinary offer, he thinks, one they could never afford otherwise. Of course, there are those endless hills that he would have to hobble up and down. Mostly, though, he thinks about Ellie and the importance of the trip to her. He would have to skip some classes and site visits, and he might not be as prepared for docent work as he would like. Then again, he thinks, she seems to understand my limitations. I have nothing to lose, and it will be a wonderful time in San Francisco.

Judith and Michael's condo is on the top floor, looking down Russian Hill to the waterfront with its tall ships at the docks and Alcatraz on a rock in the center of the Bay. Judith has decorated the condo with Tibetan art and furniture and a display of her black-and-white photographs of Tibetan people. It is a beautiful place, and Walt and Ellie sink into its atmosphere.

At this point, Walt has partial return of the functioning of his right leg, but he cannot write with his right hand. He lacks instinctive knowledge of how to hold a fork. He grips it in an unwieldy way at the very end, and eating peas or salad is a problem for him. His lip droops when he does not smile. He has trouble with sensations over about four inches of the right side of his face and continuing into his throat and right torso.

Walt and Ellie spend very full weeks touring the city and surrounding area. Ellie does all the driving, but Walt parks the car, a job that sometimes leaves him at a considerable distance from their lodgings. After about three weeks, Judith and Michael return to San Francisco, and Judith gives a party in honor of Walt and Ellie. At the party, Walt works hard to be friendly and outgoing. Judith and Michael's friends are enthusiastic about his progress. One woman, a writer, tells Ellie that she would like to write their story. She is the first of several people who ask to write about the stroke, the earthquake, and the tsunami.

Toward the end of their stay, they host their grandson Satchel for a trip to see the Dalai Lama in San Diego. They visit the aircraft carrier *Midway*, anchored in the harbor. Its warlike appearance is in marked contrast to the atmosphere surrounding the Dalai Lama, who speaks to a peace-loving crowd of 10,000 at UCSC. The Dalai Lama is very down-to-earth, and Satchel is much taken with him.

In April 2012, a cargo container washes up on a remote beach on Graham Island, British Columbia. Among camping gear and golf clubs is a Harley-Davidson motorcycle with Japanese plates. It appears the container was swept into the sea when the tsunami struck Miyagi. Peter Mark, a beachcomber, researches the plates and discovers that the owner, a former resident of the town of Yamamoto, has survived the tsunami, but has lost everything, including three family members. Quickly, Peter arranges to send the motorcycle back.

When the bike arrives, Ikuo Yokoyama, age 29, is so happy that he prepares a video thanking Peter Mark for returning his motorcycle. Apparently, this bike has withstood some of Ikuo's challenging trips, and he has real affection for it. Although it is quite rusted, he plans to restore it. Asked if he has anything to say to his bike, Ikuo laughs.

"Thanks for coming back, buddy," he says.

When Walt and Ellie return home, he prepares for docent work at the Portland Observatory. However, the information session leaves him anxious that he will not be able to speak loudly enough to deliver the pertinent information. He studies texts and writes out his talk, but he worries about the frailty of his voice. Sophie, his granddaughter, comes to his aid with a microphone attached to a karaoke player. Walt is greatly relieved.

The Portland Observatory is a popular site on the top of Munjoy Hill. Built by Captain Lemuel Moody in 1807, the Observatory is the last standing signaling station on the east coast. Because ship owners at the waterfront could not see the ocean beyond the islands, Captain Moody developed a business of signaling the waterfront about approaching ships. From the Observatory, he could see ships a day or two in advance, and his signal allowed the owners ample time to assemble the dockhands for unloading.

On the day that he is to start at the Observatory, Walt takes Sophie's karaoke machine with him. He is pleased to find, however, that he can make himself heard without it. On his first tour, he takes a small group up the seven flights of stairs of the Observatory. He is self-conscious about his voice, which to him sounds muffled and garbled. He remembers that Steve, his speech therapist, told him that his voice is really all right, so he pushes on through his hesitancy and concentrates on his next words.

His second tour of the day is a former docent who has brought his family to see the Observatory. The docent appears very competent, and he is already delivering a mini lecture as he shows his family around. While giving the introductory speech on the ground floor of the Observatory, Walt feels a threatened paralysis, and on the second floor, this paralysis gets hold of him and he cannot find the necessary words. The former docent's expression fluctuates between horror and revulsion. I've got to push on, Walt thinks. By the time he is at the third floor, he regains his speech. At the end of the tour, the docent and his family leave. He's probably unhappy with the tour, Walt tells himself, but I cannot let this experience derail my rehabilitation. I need to push on.

Floating debris from the tsunami spreads throughout the Pacific. Loggerhead sea turtles mistake plastic bags for jellyfish, and albatrosses feed plastic resin pellets to their chicks, only to have them die of starvation or ruptured organs. Debris near the surface blocks sunlight from plankton and algae below, and fish and turtles have less food.

In June 2012, on Agate Beach, Oregon, a 70-foot dock floats ashore. It is composed of concrete with metal pontoons, and the commemorative plaque shows that it is owned by the Aomori Prefecture. The dock broke loose from the port of Misawa in the tsunami and has traveled 5,000 miles across the Pacific Ocean. The Aomori Prefecture has lost three other docks, and this is the first to wash ashore; they do not want it returned.

One and a half tons of Japanese oceanic life has attached itself to the dock, and this must be scraped off and buried above the high-water mark so that it will not contaminate Oregon's ocean. Before it is removed, however, Mitch Vance, shellfish program manager for the Oregon Department of Fish and Wildlife, takes samples of the mussels, barnacles, and other shellfish clinging to the sides. Among them is a starfish that lives only in Japanese waters.

Initially, authorities cannot decide whether to tow the dock elsewhere or cut it up on the beach. In the meantime, the shores of Oregon, Washington, and British Colombia are being littered with oyster buoys, crates, parts of small refrigerators, and small fishing boats. California is spared due to spring and summer winds driving down the Oregon coast and causing an upwelling of the water.

On June 21st, Walt and Ellie try out a used boat they are thinking of buying. A 22-foot Pursuit with a 150hp Evinrude motor, the boat appears totally seaworthy, and Walt and his grandsons take it from the Yarmouth Boat Yard to their mooring at Sebasco Harbor. Before the stroke, Walt would have had no problem managing this boat, but he is relieved to turn it over to his grandsons. They drive it throughout the summer, while Walt remains a passenger.

Ellie is very busy at Sebasco, and Walt tries his hand at mowing the lawn. Unlike last year, when he did not have the strength to push the mower, now, with ample breaks, he manages it. Once again, neighbors supply him with murder mysteries, and his list of great, good, and mediocre authors continues to grow.

Through the summer, Walt continues his docent work at the Portland Observatory, and he considers becoming a docent at the Eastern Cemetery, Portland's oldest burial ground. Climbing the flights of Observatory stairs has been tough on him, but the Eastern Cemetery provides another challenge. Learning 400 years of Portland history is staggering, and he fears he will never be able to master it.

He gets copies of the books *The Description and Natural History of the Coasts of North America (Acadia)* and *The History of Portland from 1632 to 1864: With a Notice of Previous Settlements, Colonial Grants, and Changes of Government in Maine.* These are very detailed, so he settles for *Portland*, a history published by Greater Portland Landmarks in 1972. This book will have to do for his text on the stones of the Eastern Cemetery.

As Walt struggles to learn a coherent history of Portland, Ellie gets information from Judith Meyers about the Dalai Lama Center at MIT, which focuses on educating physicians, scientists, and leaders in all walks of life. The Venerable Tenzin Priyadarshi, a Tibetan Buddhist monk, has been chosen by the Dalai Lama to run the Center, and Judith knows Tenzin and is happy to introduce Ellie. Ellie is interested because the Center is teaching "Ethical Leadership for a Global Age," and the Dalai Lama considers this essential in a world so lacking in ethics. She, Judith, and Tenzin spend three hours having lunch, and he urges her to get support for teaching secular ethics in Maine schools.

In December 2012, an Internet ad suddenly appears for a condominium at Zeitler Farm, Brunswick. This property has been too expensive for Walt and Ellie, but the real estate market is at its lowest point, and up it pops in their online search. The condo is more beautiful than anything they have seen in Portland. Ellie likes it, and although she still does not know what caused Walt's stroke, he appears to get better and better. They decide they can purchase the condo, and they move to Zeitler Farm.

In fall of 2012 Walt and Ellie receive a generous gift from their daughter-in-law Sarah, who offers them her parents' lovely house in Ft. Worth for a month. Here they can relax and enjoy their twin grandchildren, Ella and Will.

In December 2012, another dock washes up in Olympic National Park in Washington. Researchers from Oregon State University, Williams College, and the Natural History Museum of Los Angeles mobilize by the beach. Dr. Steven Fradkin of the National Park Service leads the team that includes Allen Pleus, the Aquatic Invasive Species Coordinator for the Washington Fish and Wildlife Department.

The team samples the biological community present on the dock and finds 29 species native to Japan and two species the dock picked up in its journey across the Pacific. The general composition of life is similar to the dock that washed up on Agate Beach six months earlier. There are several potentially aggressive invasive species, including European blue mussel (an invader of Japan itself), Asian brown seaweed, and Asian shore crab. Like its predecessor, this dock is scraped and its exterior is torched. Several tons of sea life is buried above the high-water mark.

Walt and Ellie settle into their new home in Brunswick. It is well lighted, with spacious windows and great privacy. Walt investigates docent experiences in Brunswick and finds he might be useful at the Chamberlain Museum, the house where General Joshua Chamberlain lived most of his life. In the new condominium he prepares a space on the second floor for his writing. His syntax is far simpler than before the stroke, and he writes about action more easily than reflection, but he is making sure progress.

In the summer of 2013, after being inundated for requests to write a book about their experience, Ellie decides that a friend and writer, David Treadwell, is the person she would like to write the book. Walt agrees, and they approach David, who has not previously expressed an interest in writing their book.

"Shouldn't Walt do it?" he asks. "He's a writer."

"I understand why you say that, Dave," Walt says. "But I'm the one who least remembers the events."

"All right," David says, "but you'll have to coach me."

After getting a detailed version of the story, David lays out a proposed series of interviews with all of Walt and Ellie's children and grandchildren, plus Judith Meyers, Dr. Jordan Waldman, Dr. Joel Botler, and Steve Belanger, the speech therapist.

The only human living in the silent radioactive zone around Fukushima nuclear plant is Naota Matsumura. He has spent the last year and a half in the eerie ghost town, making do without electricity or running water.

"I don't get bored," he tells the hazmat-suited reporters who seek him out. "There are lots of animals here, so I'm never really alone."

Matsumura has become a folk hero to animal lovers around the world. He spends his days feeding 400 cows, 60 pigs, more than a hundred cats and dogs, and a female ostrich—all abandoned in the disaster.

Naota's hometown, Tomioka, a village of 16,000 eight miles from the Fukushima Daiichi nuclear plant, once boasted one of Japan's longest cherry-blossom tunnels. Now it stands empty except for a single traffic light blinking over the deserted main street. A layer of radioactive cesium particles covers everything.

Although the Japanese press does not like to mention it, police with Geiger counters prevent anyone from entering the twenty-mile-wide zone where ATMs were looted long ago. Now it is estimated that 684 million yen—8.4 million dollars—in radioactive bills now circulate in Japan.

Matsumura does not need much money because he has a generator, a stock of charcoal, and plenty of candles. He boils water for ramen and eats canned food.

"There are good sides to this tragedy. Life has become cheaper," he explains, but then adds with resignation, "With radioactivity, I think I will live until my sixties at best."

Matsumura is only able to save a small portion of the cattle left to starve in their pens.

"I'm full of rage," he says. "That's why I'm still here. I refuse to leave and let go of this anger and grief."

Daily, he is confronted with the result of this sudden evacuation—a cage of withered canaries or a calf that choked to death as it grew too large for the rope around its neck.

"People don't want to see dead animals. They would be shocked if they saw it themselves," he says.

Walt signs up to perform docent work for the Chamberlain House. His speech is pretty good except when he is anxious, so he elects to do his first supervised tour with two experienced docents. On the tour, he does not answer questions very well, and after the trial run, one of the experienced docents tells him he is not ready. The docent appears quite concerned.

"Go around with some other docents," he says. "See how they do it."

Walt nods. He has learned that he must ignore initial awkwardness and push ahead, so he goes around again with the same docents who have been concerned about him. When he finishes, despite their concerns, he signs up for his first solo docent experience. By the second tour, he is once again feeling comfortable. He tells no one related to the Chamberlain Museum that he has had a stroke.

Two years after the earthquake and tsunami the Japanese people are dissatisfied with their government's slow pace of recovery. Mortality figures have leaped to nearly 19,000, and 300,000 people are still displaced.

"I pray that the peaceful lives of those affected can resume as soon as possible," Emperor Akihito says.

Walt continues to do well. Some of his friends cannot believe he has had a stroke. Everyone, including Ellie, describe him as a miracle.

Two of the country's nuclear reactors remain offline, and half of the evacuees are from areas near the stricken Fukushima Daiichi have banded together to file a lawsuit demanding compensation from the government and the former plant owner, Tokyo Electric Power, or TEPCO.

"What I really want to have once again is 'my home,'" says Migaku Suzuki, a farmer from Rikuzentakata, who lost his new house and a son in the disaster.

Further south, in Fukushima Prefecture, other evacuees wonder if they will ever be allowed to return to their homes. Meltdowns in three reactors have spewed radiation into the soil and water, and it is not going away.

The Fukushima leak is much worse that residents have been led to believe. In August 2013, Mycle Schneider, a consultant who previously advised the French and German governments, tells the press that water is leaking out all over the site, and there are no accurate figures for radiation levels. A thousand tanks have been built for the water used to cool the plant, but these already are believed to be 85% full. Every day, 400 tons of water is added.

"The quantities of water they are dealing with are absolutely gigantic," Mr. Schneider says. "What is worse is the water leakage everywhere else—not just from the tanks. It is leaking out from the basements, it is leaking out from the cracks all over the place. Nobody can measure that."

"It is not over yet by a long shot," Dr. Ken Buesseler, senior scientist at Woods Hole Oceanographic Institution, says. "Chernobyl was in many ways a one-week fire-explosive event, nothing with this potential right on the ocean. Once it gets into the ground water, like a river flowing to the sea, you can't really stop groundwater flow."

During the summer of 2013, Walt offers docent-led tours at the Chamberlain Museum in Brunswick and the Observatory and Eastern Cemetery in Portland. Then, in the fall, he prepares for a docent experience at the Peary-Macmillan Arctic Museum at Bowdoin College. The Christies have acquired Lily, a miniature Labradoodle, and Walt and Ellie walk her every day.

Ellie is relaxing more and more. Walt is really doing well, she thinks.

He shows no signs of lack of confidence. His writing is very good, and he seems to enjoy the docent experiences. I really do think we're going to have a life after stroke.

9

Reflection, Action

Walt is growing reflective. An awareness of a deeper self now complements his "push on" mentality of the first two years of rehabilitation. He remembers being one with the world during the total solar eclipse in Alaska in 1963. Then, as he stood on a hillside, the skies darkened, and the sun became a dark penumbra. Caribou roiled and stampeded on the tundra below him. Mother grizzlies, in search of safety, ran up the slopes with babies bounding behind them. Owls, feeling the disturbance in the heavens, awoke from their slumber and circled wildly in the air. Nature stood on its head, and then, as the sun slowly reappeared, it reversed itself and fell back into its pattern.

Walt also remembers India and his first view of the Himalayas in 1995. It was a cold, crisp March day, and snow-covered peaks were shining above the Taragarh Palace. Later, they reached Dharamsala, India, high above the lush Kangra Valley, where he and Ellie brought medicines for the Tibetan Children's' Village. The next morning, they circumambulated the Dalai Lama's residence. Then, in Nepal, their journey took them over cultivated mountains where they gazed down through terraced landscapes at the tiny villages below.

Ellie has told him about her favorite author, Lama Govinda, a German scholar-artist who became a Tibetan monk and wrote a classic book, *The Way of the White Clouds*. Lama Govinda was eloquent, and his spirituality was one with the landscape of Tibet. As Walt leafs through Ellie's copy of the book, he is moved by the descriptions of the mountains and the vast sky.

Ellie, in the meantime, has assumed many of Walt's responsibilities, and she is pressed for time. She attempts to push clutter from her mind, but some piece of news always brings it back. It is over two years since the disaster, but like ocean debris, the news washes ashore and makes the events of Osaka seem like yesterday.

More than ever, Ellie feels a part of a "global community" struggling on a planet of continual change, and the mental principles taught by the Dalai Lama are her guide. She tries to be present to reality. She is aware of the moment and avoids distractions. She continually gets out of her comfort zone and examines what she has control over while letting go of what she does not. She practices gratitude because change, she finds, is the only constant truth.

One morning, she is having coffee at a little café when she bumps into an old friend, George, whom she has not seen since Walt's stroke. George asks if she knows that has had a stroke himself.

"You should talk to Liz," he says, speaking of his wife. "She's right out in the car."

Ellie finds Liz, who immediately asks her if she knows why Walt had had a stroke. Perplexed about George's condition, Liz has researched an expert physician on stroke.

"You've got to consult him," she explains. "His name is Dr. Schwamm, a Harvard trained neurologist and one of America's foremost experts on stroke and cerebrovascular disease."

Ellie is excited. For two years, she has lived with the uncertainty of the cause and therefore, the prognosis of Walt's stroke. She is eager to get Dr. Schwamm's opinion.

The tsunami debris scatters across a vast expanse of the North Pacific. The larger pieces float close to the coast of the continental U.S. and Alaska, while the smaller pieces move slowly east north of Hawaii. Around this vast pool of debris the Great Pacific Garbage Patch slowly churns.

Two years after quitting work, Walt is still learning how to retire. In his docent work, as in his early days as a psychiatrist, a few refer to him as a "guide." Writing, too, has become important, and chapter by chapter, the book is progressing. It's fun for him to evolve the plot, and the characters feel increasing alive. In the '80s, while he was full time in psychiatry, he gave up trying to write for lack of time. Now writing is like finding an old friend.

The Great Pacific Garbage Patch spins from the Eastern Garbage Patch, a gyre turning between Hawaii and California, to the West Coast Patch churning the waters near Japan. These vortexes of debris are fed by the North Pacific Subtropical Convergence Zone, which brings the warm water of the South Pacific to meet the cool water of the Arctic. The currents macerate the debris until it is like cloudy soup. Deposits many feet deep build on the ocean floor below the two patches.

During the summer of 2013, Walt and Ellie go to Boston to meet Dr. Schwamm. They find the doctor very personable, and Walt is impressed with the level of detail of Dr. Schwamm's history and physical—especially the physical, which is like the exams that Walt used to do when seeing patients with neurological complaints. Dr. Schwamm tells them that Walt's stroke came from the left side of the heart or higher, ruling out a clot from the legs. He does an ultrasound, and the carotid arteries do not point to a source, either. Dr. Schwamm suggests either a spontaneous clot in the afflicted artery of the brain or a random clot thrown by the left side of the heart.

"In any case," he explains, "you are now no more at risk for another stroke than any other seventy-year-old man."

Walt and Ellie are greatly reassured by this.

In the fall of 2013, Ellie interests high school teachers in Brunswick and Portland in the Dalai Lama Center's teaching of ethics. She works to bring the program to these schools. Walt continues his work as docent for the Chamberlain House in Brunswick. He feels a kinship with General Chamberlain, who was a hardworking man with a chivalric nature that seemed empowered by something higher. Chamberlain repeatedly transformed his house as he went from college professor to war hero, to governor, and to president of Bowdoin College. In the history of being moved, turned, and raised, the house symbolizes the turns of Walt's career in psychiatry, as well as his passion for the environment and for writing.

It is more than two years since the earthquake and tsunami, and TEPCO, the owner of Fukushima Daiichi, now admits that the plant is still leaking radioactive water into the ocean. This incenses the fishermen of Fukushima Prefecture, who must live with the ban on fishing. TEPCO states that they cannot stop the groundwater flow, which mixes with radioactive cesium and other elements and seeps out to sea.

Two months later, in the fall of 2013, the Japanese government announces they will build a wall of ice around the stricken plant. The ice barrier will take until March 2015 to construct. The Kajima Corporation will erect the 1.4-kilometer perimeter wall by sinking pipes carrying icy fluids, which will gradually freeze the ground to form a barrier of permafrost down to the bedrock 30 meters below. This will force the contaminated water to flow into the sea.

In July 2014, the Dalai Lama Center offers a program for teachers at the MIT campus. Ellie attends this program, taught by Venerable Tenzin Priyadarshi, the founding president and CEO of the Dalai Lama Center. Tenzin asks participants to engage students in a transformative process, then videotape them and produce films and reflective papers discussing the experience of the process.

Meanwhile, Walt discovers that writing a novel is more than just rehabilitation for the stroke. He writes regularly now, and chapter after chapter is completed. No longer preoccupied by his profession, he finds writing quite pleasurable.

Lily, their one-year-old Labradoodle, thoroughly enjoys other dogs, so in the late spring of 2014, when her breeder sends an e-mail saying that a six-week-old red-haired Labradoodle is without an owner because that man suddenly received a terminal diagnosis, Walt and Ellie see an opportunity. They say yes to Ruby, who is an affectionate, engaging puppy who can stand on her hind legs for a long time.

"She could be looking for a job at Barnum and Bailey," Ellie says.

Walt agrees.

Lily completely agrees, and Ruby becomes her baby.

After attending the MIT certificate program, Ellie starts working with students, teaching ethical leadership based on compassion. She works on her papers and completes the videos for MIT. A short time later, she learns that the International Symposium for Contemplative Studies will be held in Boston in the fall. The Symposium will sponsor a day-long program with the Dalai Lama Center in which the Dalai Lama himself will participate. She enrolls in the Symposium, which is filled with men and women, many of them working on Ph.D.s in various aspects of contemplative studies. At the end of November, she finishes the requirement for certification by the MIT center to teach ethical leadership.

On September 29, 2014, Jordan and Anita Waldman come to visit. The reason for their trip from San Diego is a wedding in Massachusetts, but it is also a good excuse to come to Maine. When they are sitting in the Christies' living room, Jordan reveals that the flight to Bangkok is still on his mind. Feeling very fortunate and humble, Walt listens as Ellie, Jordan, and Anita reconstruct the events of March 12, 2011. It is clear that the decision to divert and land the huge airplane was completely in Jordan's hands. Walt, much to Jordan's relief, tells him he is grateful to have had a good doctor in charge of that decision.

In December 2014, Walt finishes his Indian novel and rejoices.

"Can you believe it?" he exclaims. "After thirty years, it's finally finished."

"It's wonderful," Ellie says. "How do you feel?"

"Like a writer!" Walt says.

"Could you write *our* book?"

"I'd sure like to try."

So that morning, Walt approaches David about taking over the writing. David is very encouraging and says, "I think you can do it."

≈

In February 2015, Tokyo is evacuated because of a 6.9 quake, measured at a depth of 10 kilometers with an epicenter 210 kilometers east of the town of Miyado. The Prefecture of Ofanato in Iwate also issues an evacuation order to more than 1,350 households. However, the earthquake experts determine it is an aftershock of the 2011 quake, and no injuries are reported.

On April 9, 2015, about 160 melon-headed whales beach themselves in Hokotashi City, Ibaraki Prefecture. Tadasu Yamada, a researcher at the National Museum of Nature and Science, can find no cause for the whales' deaths. Public anxiety rises because it is common knowledge that over 100 pilot whales, a close relative of the melon-headed whales, beached themselves less than 48 hours before the 2011 quake and tsunami. Indian professor Dr. Arunachalam Kumar sees a connection between the beaching of marine mammals and earthquakes.

"It is my observation, confirmed over the years, that mass suicides of whales and dolphins that occur sporadically all over the world are in some way related to change and disturbances in the electromagnetic field coordinates and possible realignments of geotectonic plates..."

Also in April 2015, a couple of miles offshore, Oregon police, inspecting fishing licenses, find a floating 30-foot piece of a Japanese fishing trawler. Most Japanese boats that have washed up in the United

States have been shallow and light, but this craft would have been over 50 feet in length. The Oregon Parks and Recreation Department hauls the wreck into port, where it is checked for numbers to identify its origin. The authorities determine that it is the type of boat designed to haul fish, but it is not equipped to cross the ocean.

In a contained area on the vessel are several yellowtail jack fish. These fish are residents of Japan and could have been caught and stored before the tsunami or hatched from roe that was aboard when the boat went adrift. Previously, in 2013, authorities had found six live fish in the bait box of a 20-foot boat that washed up on the Washington coast. These were the first live fish from Asia that researchers had encountered.

≈

As Walt and Ellie have coffee, Walt tries to describe how the stroke and the tsunami has changed them.

"You know, the earthquake and the tsunami weren't just in 2011," he says. "Every day they just keep happening—another aftershock, another piece of debris washing up.

"Do you remember," he continues, "how we used to believe that things were happening to us personally, like fate?"

"Yes, everyone and everything in the universe is interconnected," Ellie says. "But at the same time, it is vast, impersonal, and devoid of personal meaning."

As they drink their coffee and talk, halfway around the world the earth begins to tremble.

At 11:56 a.m. Nepalese time on April 25, 2015, an earthquake strikes Nepal. It is severe and very shallow, the worst disaster to strike Nepal since the 1934 Nepal-Bihar earthquake.

10

Kathmandu, Dalai Lama's Advice

On April 25, 2015, Judith Meyers is giving a birthday party for Michael. They have moved from their beautiful condominium in San Francisco to an interesting frame house in Rye, New Hampshire. Judith has invited some old friends who have worked in Nepal and Tibet and some new friends that she and Michael have met since they came to New Hampshire.

On the morning of the party, Ellie begins to reminisce. She thinks about her journey with Ginny to Tibet and about Alexandra David-Neel, the woman who inspired her. Alexandra David-Neel was an amazing woman. In the 1920s, disguised as a man, she traveled far onto the Tibetan plateau to visit Lhasa. Ellie read her book, *My Journey to Lhasa*, and was excited by her courage.

Then Ginny and I go to Tibet, she thinks, and I come back and marry Walt. Seven years later, he and I trek the Himalayan mountains of Nepal and northern India, and then we go back to Dharamsala for the first class in English for Tibetan medicine at Men-Tsee-Khang, the Dalai Lama's medical school. In 1997, we host the Dalai Lama's personal physician, Dr. Tenzin Choedrak, and his medical team in Maine on their first tour in the U.S.

"Ellie," Walt calls from the kitchen. "There's been an earthquake in Nepal."

Later, as they drive to the party, they listen intently to reports of the earthquake. It just happened last night, and the casualty figures are preliminary, but they are predicted to be in the many thousands. The radio reports that a snow-slide has covered much of the Base Camp at Mt. Everest, where hundreds of climbers and Sherpas are preparing for this year's assault on the summit. Before the avalanche, several parties had already left the camp and are ascending the mountain. Their fate is unknown, but for those in Base Camp, the reports are grim. A wall of snow has rolled right over them, pushing people and tents hundreds of feet and burying them in deep snow. From the USA, the dead include a Base Camp medic, a Google executive, and a documentary filmmaker.

Ellie and Walt listen with sober attention. Although it is a beautiful day, the handsome colonial houses with their old stone walls cannot distract their attention from the radio. Kathmandu is very special to Ellie. She has been there four times, twice with Ginny and twice with Walt at the beginning and the end of their trekking experiences. She imagines people amidst slabs of fallen buildings, collapsed temples, and sacred stupas turning to dust. The radio reports that as many as 20,000 foreign nationals are in Nepal, including a few from Maine. A son from Portland and daughter from Alaska are frantically trying to contact their mother, who was hiking alone in a devastated area.

Walt and Ellie reach Judith and Michael's house by the tidal estuary, and Michael greets them and shows them their room. Another couple has also come a distance for the party and plans on staying the night, as well. Ken, the husband, greets Ellie and Walt along with his young daughter. His wife, Sienna, is upstairs listening to broadcast reports of the quake.

Ken and Sienna both teach at Dartmouth. Sienna is an anthropologist with a background in Tibetan medical studies, and Ken is an artist who teaches in her department. They have spent several years in Nepal and are tremendously invested in the Nepalese people. Sienna appears and disappears throughout the course of the evening, always to check on Nepal and the earthquake. She is unable to rest out of concern that friends who remain in Nepal may be in danger. Ellie instantly feels a bond with her.

The other guests seem able to put the quake aside for a few hours and let Michael have his birthday party. At the end of the evening, the only people remaining are Sienna and Ken, Judith and Michael, and Ellie and Walt. Immediately, the earthquake becomes the topic of discussion.

Sienna and Ken explain that the Nepalese people are very poor. Years of political strife have left the country destitute, and the murder of the royal family has compounded it. Also, the mountainous terrain is precarious, with many landslides occurring as a result of the quake. Over the next few weeks, many more are expected. Thus, getting medical supplies and food to the remote villages is a challenge. Many villages are totally buried beneath these slides—and all this at the start of monsoon season.

The Gorkha earthquake, named for the district of its epicenter, is not Mega-Thrust 9+, but it is shallower and therefore more dangerous in mountainous country where the risk of landslides is very high. The epicenter is near the village of Barpak, 80 kilometers northwest of Kathmandu, but it causes landslides as far away as Mt. Everest, 160 kilometers to the northeast. Tremors are felt in the neighboring Indian states of Bihar, Uttar Pradesh, Assam, West Bengal, Sikkim, Uttarakhand, Odisha, Andhra Pradesh, Gujarat, and in the capital region around New Delhi. Many buildings are reported toppling in Bihar, and there is minor cracking of buildings as far south as the state of Kerala. Tremors are also felt in Tibet, Pakistan, and Bhutan.

Walt has not thought much about the risk of landslides. When he and Ellie trekked in Nepal twenty years before, the hillsides looked stable. Since that time, however, Nepal has built many roads in the northern hills. These roads offer passage to the hordes of climbers who have come to scale Mt. Everest, but now whole villages are buried where these new roads were built.

The following morning, Walt and Ellie say goodbye to their hosts and to Sienna and Ken. They are anxious to get home and see Kathmandu on the television. When they arrive, a copy of the e-mail Sienna and Ken sent to friends is there.

Dear Family, Friends, and Colleagues,

Yesterday at noon local time, a massive 7.8 magnitude earthquake hit the Himalayan country of Nepal. As of this writing, the official death toll is over 2,500, but the actual casualties from this catastrophic event are orders of magnitude greater than this number. These deaths are occurring not only in the capital city, but also across Nepal's rural hill and mountain communities.

In the past 24 hours, the country has experienced more than 80 aftershocks, including two additional major quakes in the Kathmandu Valley and northeast of the capital. Avalanches in the Everest region have resulted in the death of mountain climbers, both foreign and local. Landslides further threaten homes and communities throughout the country, particularly north and east of the Kathmandu Valley. Entire villages have turned to rubble overnight. World Heritage sites have toppled. The human loss is impossible to calculate. The Nepali people and the nation as a whole are experiencing this tragedy in the wake of a brutal 10-year civil war (1996–2006) and now, nearly a decade of fragile peace and political instability.

Although Nepal is a half a world away, it is a place close to the hearts and minds of many of you, and certainly of us. We are deeply concerned, saddened, and moved to action by these events. The work of immediate relief—including for the provision of water, food, and shelter—is essential. So too are efforts toward rebuilding and resilience over the long term. In the coming weeks, access to water, food, and housing will continue to be important. As the monsoon begins in early summer, this will bring with it further challenges to everything from clean water to landslides and rebuilding efforts. The fact that approximately 3 million of Nepal's able-bodied men and women are abroad working as wage laborers contributes to the complexity of rebuilding, particularly in rural areas.

In solidarity with the strong and suffering people of Nepal.

Namaste,

Sienna and Ken

On television, Ellie and Walt watch video of the destruction in Kathmandu. As Ellie feared, the images are horrendous. Surrounded by mountains, Kathmandu is a bowl of soft sedimentary rock, and the quake jounces the centuries-old buildings up and down and then destroys them. Gone are the World Heritage sites of Bhaktapur Durbar Square, Changu Narayan Temple, and Swayambuhunath Stupa—all places that Ellie saw with Ginny in 1988 and Walt and Ellie visited together in 1995. The wounded and dead are everywhere.

At first, crews can only get cameras to Kathmandu and the Base Camp of Everest. At the Base Camp, rescue parties are still trying to dig out those who perished in the avalanche. The rest of the climbers are sadly preparing to go home, for the earthquake has put an end to climbing for this season. Radio communication has been made with some of the outlying villages, although some are silent and appear to be completely covered by slides.

Walt ponders landslides. There seem to be hundreds of them in Nepal. The 2011 Japanese earthquake started under the ocean and produced very few landslides. The tsunami did enormous damage, but then retreated … but in Nepal the threat of landslides continues. Thousands of acres of rock, gravel, and mud have been jarred loose and are poised to fall at any time.

"I never dreamed the land was so unstable," Ellie says. "When Ginny and I were in Nepal in 1988, and when you and I trekked in 1995, I never gave landslides a thought."

"The Maoists were organizing then," Walt says. "After we left, there was a long civil war. The extensive road-building in the north must have started after that. The risk of slides is much greater now."

The daughter of the mother from Maine comes goes to Nepal from Alaska to look for her mother in Langtang Village. She arrives to terrible destruction.

"There was unfathomable damage, destruction, and loss," she states. "There's nothing good to say about it. It's very difficult to share.

"By the time we got there, it really seemed the people were

resigned," she says. "They were rummaging through the destruction, wanting to find bodies and any material things they could use" to survive and rebuild as best they could.

On May 15, 2015, another earthquake occurs with an epicenter between Mt. Everest and Kathmandu. It is a 6.6 quake that kills more than 200 people and injures 2,500. This earthquake occurs along the same fault line as the 7.8 Gorkha quake, but is further to the east. Experts consider it an aftershock.

The international press coverage of the mother from Maine elicits an e-mail from the United Kingdom. A woman hiker saw her on the day before the earthquake.

"She saw this beautiful woman walking down toward Langtang Village as they were walking up toward Kyanjing Gompa with all these kids surrounding her," the son reports. The hiker thought the woman was a teacher or an aid worker.

"It was no surprise that she was surrounded by children," the son says. "She was youthful and vibrant. She had a very special connection with children."

He explains that above Langtang Village a huge sheet of ice broke free from the surrounding peaks, triggering an avalanche a mile and a half wide that buried the village of 400 local people and as many as 100 foreigners. This was the Maine woman's fourth trip to Nepal since her first trip in 1998, when she was changed by the experience.

"I think it was a monumental spiritual event for her," her daughter says.

Walt reads the newspaper story about the woman and realizes she is a lot like Ellie.

"This could have been you," he says.

"I know," Ellie responds. "Ginny and I were often surrounded by children."

It has been a month since the deadly earthquake in Nepal. Relief workers plead for urgent help for hundreds of thousands of people still living under tarps. They fear that the monsoon rains, due to begin in weeks, could trigger more landslides, damage villages, and cut off roads. Without dry shelter, the rain will also bring sickness and disease. Some communities may experience freezing temperatures and snow, as well. The mountainous countryside is a challenge, and humanitarian response is, to date, insufficient.

On May 25, 2015, a powerful earthquake shakes Tokyo, causing temporary suspension of the area's train system and closing of the runways at Narita International Airport. The 5.5 magnitude quake, centered on the northern part of Saitama Prefecture, does not cause any immediate reports of damage. However, for a few seconds, Tokyo holds its breath.

Then, on May 30, 2015, a powerful 7.8 magnitude earthquake strikes Tokyo. Three hundred kilometers away on Hahajima Island, near the epicenter, a Buddhist shrine sways wildly.

"This was very big quake...the shaking was felt over a broad area... fortunately, because it was deep, there is little danger of tsunami," Naoki Hirata, of the University of Tokyo's earthquake research center, says.

But the Japanese are worried. As predicted, since 2011 the earthquake epicenters are moving closer to them.

In Nepal the monsoons are starting.

"I still want to do everything we can for Nepal and Langtang," the daughter of the mother from Maine says.

"The last picture of our mother offers great solace and peace, as it represents our mother's true serenity and beauty in an equally beautiful surrounding," the son and daughter write.

On the day that his mother was due to fly back to the States, the son's wife gives birth to a baby girl.

It is the last of May, and Ellie and Walt are having coffee.

"A friend sent me an e-mail this morning," Ellie says. "It's a quote from the Dalai Lama."

Ellie gets up and goes to her laptop. She returns with a picture of the Dalai Lama. His words are written across the page:

We can let the circumstances of our lives harden us so that we become increasingly resentful and afraid, or we can let them soften us, and make us kinder. You always have the choice.

Biographical Notes

Ellie and Walt Christie met in 1982 when he was giving a lecture on the evolution of consciousness. Walt was a hospital-based psychiatrist, and Ellie was teaching mind-body medicine to family medicine residents. Ellie first traveled to Nepal and Tibet in 1988, a few months before they were married. In 1995, they made a trip to India and Nepal and another one to Dharamsala, India, to take the first course in English at Men-Tsee-Khang, the Dalai Lama's medical school. The stroke in 2011 was totally unforeseen.

Bibliography

Note: Entries are listed in the order their relevance within each chapter.

Chapter 1

Ehrlich, Gretel. *Facing the Wave: A Journey in the Wake of the Tsunami.* First Vintage Books Edition, 2013, Chapter 10.

Delta pilot's story retrieved from www.flightglobal.com/ … / flight/ … /2011/ … /delta-pilot-recount …

"Death, people missing set to top 1,600": Edano, *The Japan Times,* March 13, 2011.

Chapter 2

"2011 Tohoku earthquake and tsunami" (2014/2/6). Retrieved from www.wikipedia.org.

"Plate-born quake 'shifts Earth's axis 10 cm'": *The Japan Times,* March 13, 2011.

Chapter 3

"Sports stars grapple with bad news": *The Japan Times,* March 13, 2011.

Chapter 4

Ibid.: other reports on the Tohoku earthquake and tsunami.

Chapter 5

Ibid.

"Russian Far East: Kamchatka: Petropavlovsk-Kamchatsky" (2014/7/7). Retrieved from www.wikipedia.org.

Toro, Ross. "Tracking Japan's Tsunami Debris" (infographic). *Live Science* 2012/6/25. Retrieved from www.livescience.com/21067 - japan-tsunami-tracking.

Chapter 8

Reuters: "Japan still coping with human, economic costs of tsunami one year later" (2011/3/10). Retrieved from www.nationalpost. co/ …./blog.

Newcomb, Tim. "What the Waves Brought: Japanese Tsunami Debris in North America, World," *Time Magazine*. Retrieved from www.newsfeed.time.com.

"70-foot dock from Japan washes up on Oregon beach" (2012/6/6). Retrieved from www.nydailynews.com.

Northwest Fisheries Science Center, 2014: "Coastal Upwelling" retrieved from www.nwfsc.noaa.gov/.

"Japanese dock washes ashore in the Olympic National Park, Washington; Biota on Japanese Tsunami Debris" (2013/1/15). Retrieved from www.blog.oregonstate.edu/floatingdock/2013/01.

Kennedy, Helen. "Japan earthquake and tsunami: One man stays to tend animals left in the radioactive zone," *New York Daily News*, March 12, 2012. Retrieved from www.nydailynews.com.

Kurtenbach, Elaine. "Recovery slow as Japan marks 2 years since tsunami" (2013/3/11). Retrieved from www.news.yahoo.com.

Marshall, Michael. "Fukushima residents may never go home," *New Scientist*, August 8, 2011. Retrieved from www.newscientist.com.

Coghlan, Andy. "Japan with build wall of ice to stem Fukushima leak": *New Scientist*, September 2013, Retrieved from www.newscientist.com.

Chapter 9

Govinda, Lama Anagarika. *The Way of White Clouds*. London: Rider and Company, 1977.

"Great Pacific Garbage Patch": Encyclopedic Entry, *National Geographic*, 2015. Retrieved from www.education.nationalgeographic.com.

Ocean Conservatory, April 14, 2015: "Tsunami Debris 101" retrieved from www.oceanconservatory.org/...debris/tsunami-debris-.

McCurry, Justin. "Fukushima radiation leaks reach deadly new high," *The Guardian*, September 4, 2013. Retrieved from www.the-guardian.com.

Coghlan, Andy. "Japan will build wall of ice to stem Fukushima leak": *New Scientist*, September 3, 2013. Retrieved from www.newscientist.com/special/fukushima-crisis.

Marshall, Michael. "Fukushima leaks will keep fisheries closed": *New Scientist*, August 6, 2013. Retrieved from www.newscientist.com/.../dn23998-fukushima leaks will k...

"Japan earthquake: Tsunami alert lifted, seismologists say quake was an 'aftershock' from 2011 disaster": ABC wire, February 16, 2015. Retrieved from www.abc.net.au/.../tsunami-alert-lifted...

"160 Beached Whales May Be a Japanese Earthquake Warning": *Mysterious Universe*, April 4, 2015. Retrieved from www.mysteriousuniverse.org/.../160-beached-whales-may-be-a-japanese-earth...

Izadi, Elahe. "Boat likely destroyed in 2011 Japanese tsunami turns up in Oregon with live fish still aboard": *The Washington Post*, April 10, 2015. Retrieved from www.washingtonpost.com/.../boat-likely-destroyed-in...

Chapter 10

David-Neel, Alexandra. *My Journey to Lhasa*, Boston: Beacon Press, 1988.

United Nations, May 25, 2015: "Nepal: With monsoon season nearing, UN races humanitarian relief to quake-affected communities." Retrieved from www.un.org/apps/news/story.asp?NewsID=50958.

March, Stephanie. "Nepal earthquake: Monsoon season threatens supply of relief as thousands still living without shelter": ABC wire, May 24, 2015. Retrieved from www.abc.net.au/ … /nepalese-still … sh …

Fujikawa, Megumi. "Tokyo Rattled by Earthquake": *The Wall Street Journal*, May 25, 2015. Retrieved from www.wsj.com/ … / tokyo-rattled-by-eartthquake-1432 …

"M8.5 earthquake strikes near Ogasawara islands": *Japan Today*, May 30, 2015. Retrieved from www.japantoday.com/ … /m8-5-earethquake-strikes-near-ogas …

Russell, Eric. "Family of Augusta woman acknowledges her death in Nepal earthquake": *Portland Press Herald*, June 9, 2015. Retrieved from www.pressherald.com/ … /family-of-mainer-dawn-h